SOUTH HOLLAND PUBLIC LIBRARY

3 1350 00323 3824

W9-AVD-258

DISCARD

SOUTH HOLLAND PUBLIC LIBRARY
708/331-5262
M-Th. 10-9, Fri. 10-6, Sat. 10-5
www.southhollandlibrary.org

The
POWER
of a
WOMAN
WHO
LEADS

Gail M. Hayes

HARVEST HOUSE PUBLISHERS
EUGENE, OREGON

All Scripture quotations are taken from the *Holy Bible,* New Living Translation, copyright © 1996, 2004. Used by permission of Tyndale House Publishers, Inc., Wheaton, IL 60189 USA. All rights reserved.

Author photo by Doug Hayes Photography

Cover by Dugan Design Group, Bloomington, Minnesota

Published in association with The Steve Laube Agency, LLC, 5025 N. Central Ave., #635, Phoenix, Arizona, 85012.

THE POWER OF A WOMAN WHO LEADS

Copyright © 2013 by Gail M. Hayes
Published by Harvest House Publishers
Eugene, Oregon 97402
www.harvesthousepublishers.com

Library of Congress Cataloging-in-Publication Data
   Hayes, Gail M.
   The power of a woman who leads / Gail M. Hayes.
      p. cm.
   ISBN 978-0-7369-4936-1 (pbk.)
   ISBN 978-0-7369-4937-8 (eBook)
   1. Christian women—Religious life. 2. Self-actualization (Psychology)—Religious aspects—Christianity. 3. Self-actualization (Psychology) in women 4. Leadership—Religious aspects—Christianity. I. Title.
   BV4527.H394 2013
   248.8'43—dc23   2012027224

DISCARD
3 1350 00323 3824

All rights reserved. No part of this publication may be reproduced, stored in a retrieval system, or transmitted in any form or by any means—electronic, mechanical, digital, photocopy, recording, or any other—except for brief quotations in printed reviews, without the prior permission of the publisher.

Printed in the United States of America

13 14 15 16 17 18 19 20 21 / BP-JH / 10 9 8 7 6 5 4 3 2 1

To Inez Riley McClain,
who taught me to stand and refuse to accept defeat,
to find joy in the midst of sorrow,
to love in the face of intolerance and hatred,
to see beauty even in unsightly places,
and to lead even when others plan a mutiny.
She pushed aside her own dreams so that I could be who I have become.
She passed on the flame and ignited leadership's torch within me.

*So all of us who have had that veil removed can see
and reflect the glory of the Lord. And the Lord—
who is the Spirit—makes us more and more like
him as we are changed into his glorious image.*

2 Corinthians 3:18

Contents

1

In the Beginning…

*If you want to see what eagles see, you must be willing
to do what eagles do. You must embrace bravery and
soar while understanding the risk. You must have
no fear of heights, no fear of flying, no fear of peril or
of the hunt. You must be willing to swoop down into
danger's valley and capture your prey. You must become
a warrior-leader. You must also understand that warrior
leaders, like eagles, get to keep what they capture.*

From the beginning of time, men have always known that they have the power to make decisions. Even as far back as the Garden of Eden, people were making decisions that would influence the future of all humanity. When God put Adam in the garden, He made a decision so critical to the survival of mankind that without it, no one would exist. He knew that it was not good for man to be alone and that he needed help to live out his purpose and fulfill his destiny. So the Creator of the universe made a powerful decision to create a helper for Adam who could handle monumental projects and become known as the master multitasker.

This helper could make snap decisions without hesitation and carry heavy loads without complaining. This helper could have a child in the morning, prepare lunch at noon, and work in the fields at night. This helper could sense danger before it arrived and wrestle it to the ground once it appeared while nursing her infant. This helper could go without food or sleep for days and yet still have the energy to defeat a nation.

This helper could cross a desert on foot and, with the sand still clinging to the bottoms of her feet, enter a throne room with the presence of a queen. She could do all these things and still be vulnerable enough to need Adam's protection, all while watching his back better than the fiercest of warriors.

But God created this helper so complex and so multifaceted that even today, her thoughts and actions still befuddle the mind of man. Yet without her influence, man would be lost. God created this helper and everything on earth changed. The identity of this helper is easy for us to see. God called her good. I call her sister. She is me. She is you. She is woman.

Leading from the Beginning

"You're doing a great job, Adam. I'm proud of you," God said as He and Adam walked through the garden. The wind tickled his cheeks with its soft fingers and Adam relaxed as his feet swept through the thick, green carpet of grass. The cherry blossom perfume was intoxicating, and Adam breathed in the fragrance as he stuck his chest out with pride.

"Yes, and thanks goes to You, Lord. You've taught me everything I know, and I love working here," said Adam. But God knew that it was just a matter of time before Adam would become lonely. He knew that His daily visits would not always be enough, and before long Adam would be yearning for something more. God knew because He placed that need within Adam when He created him.

Adam would soon become lonely and long for something he did not yet know about. He would still need his daily walk with God, but this second need would complete his life.

"Adam, I need you to do something for me," God said as the cool breeze of the day danced around them.

"What is it, Lord? Anything You ask, I will do," said Adam as he slowed his pace and turned to face God.

"Well, Adam," God said. Everything in the garden grew silent, holding its breath, waiting for Him to speak again. "I need you to name all the animals here in the garden." He continued walking.

"I can do that, Lord! When do we start?" Adam asked as he ran to catch up with God. He was so excited that he nearly tripped over a giant ruby embedded in the garden pathway.

"Let's start now," said God, and He turned and motioned for the first animal to come before Adam.

When Adam saw the animal, it was as if everything God had taught him leaked out through his ears. His mind went completely blank. This was a strange-looking creature, and he realized that this was going to be more difficult than he had originally thought. As hard as he tried, all the words seemed trapped in a vault bolted shut with this project's newness.

Adam stood before this creature and lost the ability to even think. He did not want to disappoint God and felt helpless to do what He had asked him to do. Adam began to question whether or not he could perform this task. This was different from anything God had asked him to do in the past.

He dropped his head and rounded his shoulders. He became unsteady on his feet. Then, suddenly, he experienced something he did not understand. He felt the veil of discouragement drape its chilly arms around him. This chilly veil began a slow descent over his spirit and Adam, for the first time in his life, was at a loss for words. All he could do was stand before God with his head bowed while trying to keep his balance. He felt a strange tingly sensation stinging his cheeks. He wiped his face and felt an unfamiliar wetness. He wept.

As God looked into his eyes something miraculous happened. Adam's rib cage began to vibrate. It shook with such force that it nearly threw him to the ground.

And then Adam heard something he had never heard before. He heard a voice so sweet that it nearly took his breath away. This voice caused such a stirring in Adam that he almost forgot what he was supposed to be doing. He could focus on nothing but this marvelous voice. Then the voice did something that surprised Adam. It began giving Adam instructions.

"That creature looks like its name should be monkey, sweetheart," the voice said, sending tremors through Adam's ribs.

"Monkey, Lord!" Adam shouted to the Lord with a voice filled with authority.

"And this one looks like a giraffe. Oh, and there's a pig, and look at the donkey, and that must be a dog. I like the sound of that. What do you think? Oh, and look at the cat and the bird. Yippee! Look at that cow and chicken. That one is hopping so we can call him kangaroo. This is so much fun I can hardly stand it! I just love helping you name these creatures," said the voice, hardly taking a breath as the animals continued to come before Adam. As each animal approached the voice gave Adam a name. Adam in turn announced the name to God. They developed a rhythm that appeared as natural as the marriage of the clouds and the rain.

After days of naming animals and all the creatures he could see, Adam could barely stand. Fatigue embraced him and caused his knees to weaken. As he sat on the ground, sleep called his name and the weight of his eyelids nearly blinded him. His rib cage was so sore that he dared not open his eyes to see another animal for fear the voice would give him another command. He could hear the voice giggling and talking at full force, but all he wanted to do was sleep.

God is a God of mercy. He could see what was happening and He took pity on Adam. He allowed a deep sleep to fall upon him. It was so deep that nothing could have woken him except God. With the voice still talking and Adam's rib cage still vibrating, God knew that it was time to unveil His next creation to the garden.

With sleep's arms embracing him, Adam had no idea what was about to unfold. As slumber had her way with Adam, God gently opened his rib cage, released the voice, and gave it a new home. He gave it a body that was comparable to Adam's body. He knew that it was now time to present Adam with a gift. All the elements of creation were now present to see the beauty of this gift. God waited until He knew that Adam and the voice could work well together before unveiling her to the world. He waited until Adam and the voice proved that by naming the animals together, they could lead together.

The voice that so mesmerized Adam was someone we all know. Her name resounds through the corridors of our feminine spirits and ignites our hearts. She was our sister. She was and is *woman*. She was a natural-born leader and her name was Eve. She was the first leader and she knew something that many of us are just discovering. She understood who she was and she understood her power. She was born to lead!

Leading Is a Part of Who We Are

Even in biblical days, women held leadership positions. They were rulers. They managed large households. They judged. They saved their families from death. They led armies. They lobbied and changed laws. They loved. They married. They had children. They trained rulers. They imparted wisdom. They did everything imaginable to run a society and craft civilization.

They stepped into history and wore the mantle of leadership with grace, dignity, and strength. They understood that they had authority to do what appeared to be the impossible. They understood that when given the opportunity to act, they *could* act. They were unafraid and stood in the burning path of leadership and allowed it to have its way with their lives.

Now it's your turn. As a woman today, you can also do great things that will shake nations and change lives. But the challenge is to be unafraid and step into your destiny without hesitation. Timing is critical, for most situations require decisive action. The question is—what will you do when leadership calls your name? How will you respond when it arrives and holds up the mirror of purpose, waiting for you to acknowledge that the one whose reflection is staring back at you is the one uniquely called to the task at hand?

Will you run and hide? Will you question it? Will you dissect and inspect the components and then snub the opportunity? Or will you willingly embrace its fire and accept all that comes with it? How you respond to these questions will determine whether or not you will live with the frustration of missed opportunities. Your answers will either catapult you to destiny or cause you to live with regret.

Many of our sisters understood that they had authority granted by God to do what appeared to be impossible, and they did it well. Now, their stories echo through the halls of history, reminding us of who we are and what we've been called to do. They remind us that decisions made eons ago prepared the way for our coming. Through the telling of their stories and whispering of their memories, they remind us that we stand on shoulders bigger than our own and we too must step up and make decisions to set the stage for future generations. They remind us that were born to lead.

Power

Many women seem uncomfortable with the word. Although we use it freely in our everyday lives, many women would rather say that they use *influence*. Why does the word *power* seem to frighten most women? Most of us have no problem exercising our power, especially when it comes to protecting our families and assets, but we do face challenges when others call us powerful.

We would rather be called *influential*. Influence is as intangible as wind but just as powerful as any tornado. Until we come face-to-face with our God-given power and embrace it, it will not embrace us. We must make the first move.

In order for us to walk in power, we must first become comfortable with power. In other words, it is okay for a woman to have power. It okay for us to exercise that power. We do it every day and don't even realize it. When we give our children instructions, we use power. When we let our husbands know our needs, we use power. When we give our friends counsel, we use our power. We are powerful and it is time we accepted that.

In the next chapter you will take the Leadership Style Inventory. It will help you discover your leadership style and show you how beautifully you use your power. It is a tool designed to help you walk in liberty and see that you were born to lead!

Natural Leaders

Women are natural leaders. Take a look at almost any aspect of our society and you can see feminine fingerprints. Anyone can see the impact of femininity in the lives of our families, our friends, and our relationships. There is not another creature on the face of the earth that touches, loves, changes, or influences like a woman. It may be difficult to grasp, but we are just that powerful and just that fabulous. And just think—God did this by design!

But we have an enemy who does not want us to walk in destiny. He understands that we are powerful and this is one of reasons that he hates us. He understands that once we set our minds on something, it becomes our focus. Once it becomes our focus, it becomes our mission. Once it becomes our mission, we go on the hunt. We will not relinquish the hunt until we capture our prey, until we complete our mission.

So what force does our enemy use to keep us from understanding the power of our focus? He is the master of distractions. He knows that if we become distracted, we become discouraged. If we become discouraged, we become disarmed. If we become disarmed, we become disconnected. When we feel disconnected, isolation's icy darts sting us.

When we become isolated, we are vulnerable to attacks. These attacks infuse the core of our femininity with toxicity. They make us question our very purpose. Once the attacks begin, we strike out and attack other women, many of whom are innocent of any wrongdoing. We make them blameless victims of our pain. We abandon our wounded and leave them defenseless against the next wave of the enemy's attack. All this results from being caught in isolation's web.

Many of us are also performance-driven and love the feeling of accomplishment. Once we start a project and see it through to its completion, we experience an inner glow that ignites our well-being. Distraction knows that if we tap into this God-given power surge we regain our focus. This inner glow causes us to look around for other projects left unfinished. This is the time he sets in motion his distraction machine.

His machine has no power if we understand the *Identity, Purpose, Destiny* principle. Once we discover our identity, we can grasp our purpose. Once we grasp our purpose, we can step into our destiny. Nothing can change how God sees us. Nothing can remove us from His love, acceptance, or power—not what people say about us, not what we think of ourselves, and not even our enemy and his tactics. The only thing that separates us from God is sin. But because of His love for us, He even forgives us of sin when we ask.

He created us for greatness and to rule and reign. He created us to have a huge impact on the world. He created us to lead.

Let's Begin the Journey

Close your eyes and imagine that parked in front of you is the car of your dreams. This car has called your name for years and yet you've never had the nerve to even do a test drive. It is your favorite model and color and although you have not touched it, you know that to drive it would be a life-changing experience.

You see a document taped to the driver's window. As you examine it, you can hardly believe what you see. It is the title stating that the vehicle is paid in full and it is yours. You cannot imagine anyone giving you such an extravagant gift but somehow, as a leader, you understand that if you accept it there must be a cost of some kind involved.

Pushing surprise aside, you decide to open the door. Your fingertips caress the handle like a classical guitarist strokes the strings on his favorite instrument. With one smooth click, the door glides open. Perhaps one little ride won't hurt. You can always give the car back, right?

Your thoughts buzz like bees near a hive. Excitement lets you know that you are about to experience what you once thought impossible. You lean inside and inhale the scent of the vehicle's interior. Your thoughts stop their buzzing in response to the new car smell and the sight of luxury.

In the midst of all of your personal excitement, you notice that there are several other vehicles parked on the lot. You watch as smiling, nodding people surround the cars. But there are also several people who appear to be reluctant. They walk around the cars shaking their heads with arms folded across their chests, as if to say that this opportunity is not for them. It's as if they believe that this is all too good to be true and they will not be caught in a trap set for destruction.

But as a woman on a mission you have a different mindset. You are unafraid of the unknown and you are looking for something different from your normal activities. You believe that this presentation may be a part of what you seek. Your focus guides you back to your reason for being in the lot. You do not have time to wonder about what others may or may not be thinking or feeling. Before you is something you call a *mission*. And your mission is to drive this car!

Now, imagine sliding into a leather seat so supple that it conforms to the shape of your body. It is soft but it is sturdy enough to hold your body weight. It is also so sensitive to you and your environment that it automatically heats when you feel cold and cools when the air around you becomes warm. It is a delicious extravagance and like nothing you have ever experienced.

While adjusting to the opulence, you touch a button on the control panel and music embraces you. The sound caresses your eardrums as the system weaves the volume and tone into the fabric of melody. It fills the vehicle and beckons you to relax and enjoy the coming journey.

You survey the control panel and see the ignition button. When you push it, you can hear the engine purr like a giant cat that has just devoured a savory meal. With your foot on the brake, you shift into drive and feel the engine and gears begin a magical waltz as you pull out onto the open road. This is beyond driving. This is a lyrical voyage that soothes a longing that you have felt for some time. It reminds you of how you feel when you finish an important project. You relax and let the music take control.

Driving this high-performance vehicle is more than an experience. It is a calling. Although everyone on the lot was invited to take a test drive, not everyone was willing. Not everyone was prepared to take the risk. Most people appeared to be afraid of the power, speed, and, contrary to what some might tell you, the luxury. Many people walked away thinking that this type of driving experience was just not for them.

Still others lingered while taking a more detailed look at the car and hoped they could gather enough courage to take possession of it. What they soon came to realize was that if they hesitated, they would miss their opportunity. By the time they decided to participate, another had taken their place and their car. They learned that this was not a drive for those plagued by fear and indecision.

But you are different. You were unafraid when the opportunity came your way because you knew that this was the right vehicle. You also believed that you could drive it with precision. This opportunity ignited something within you that you cannot explain. This vehicle had every feature that you imagined and above all else, it captured you.

From the moment you touched the ignition switch, you understood that this would be a ride like no other you had taken. You knew without being told that you were about to experience something different and that life as you knew it would never be the same. You readied yourself for adventure. You and your vehicle found a rhythm that can only be described as musical. You are the conductor of a finely tuned orchestra of mechanical genius that plays your personal theme song.

But there are still questions lingering in your mind. Where are you going and what are you supposed to do when you get there? These questions would usually cause someone to stop and investigate, but you have a different mindset. The unknown is not unfamiliar to you. You have conquered many unknown territories before.

The engine purrs as you and the accelerator move in harmony. You accelerate and this purr becomes a growl and your giant cat moves with immense power over the open plain of the roadway. The tires hug the curves and then release them again to the chase as you turn into each straightaway. It's a feeling one finds difficult to explain. It can only be described as euphoric, especially when you drive the right vehicle the right way.

The road flows beneath you like melted chocolate. You can see it winding like a dark ribbon as it cuts a wavy trail through the landscape. You have no idea where you are headed. You only know that the journey is one you must take and that this is the vehicle designed to get you there. You understand the power of having the right equipment to get the job done.

After riding for a while, you notice that the fuel gauge is nearly empty. Fingers point and eyes stare as you pull into the gas station and step out to fill the tank. You attract attention and soon learn that the stares and finger pointing come with the territory. A smile overtakes you and pulls the corners of your mouth upward as you adjust your sunglasses. You did not ask to be in the spotlight. The spotlight has chosen you.

As you finish pumping your gas, you see a long line of cars that resemble your own pulling into the station. It seems odd that there would be so many cars of the same model and color at one location but instead of taking time to investigate, you dismiss the scene. Your main focus is getting back into your car because you don't want to miss a moment of driving time. You get on the road without noticing that the line of cars has followed you.

You decide to take the scenic route near the ocean. The breeze dancing across the waves sends a peaceful flow through the car—so strong that you slow down just to take in the view. Looking in the rearview mirror, you spot the same line of cars you saw earlier driving just behind you. As you take the exit for the ocean view roadway, you notice that the cars follow you.

Every turn you take, they take. Every curve you overtake, they overtake. Every movement you make, they seem to make. Their behavior is disturbing because they all appear to have vehicles similar to your own but you did not see anyone else take owner-ship of a vehicle while at the lot. Concern sweeps his cloudy mist over your spirit because you know that something about this situa-tion is just not right.

Frustrated with the mystery, you pull onto the side of the road. All the other cars do the same. You hesitate before getting out of your car but decide not to allow fear to rule your existence. The cir-cumstances are alarming but you have had enough. You must con-front these drivers.

When you get out of your car, all the other drivers do the same. They approach and encircle you before you've had the chance to speak. You want to run but that same inner peace that led you to take possession of your vehicle touches you. You can see their con-fused looks and you can hear the alarm in their voices. During the conversation you also discover that they have been following you because they believe you have answers to all their questions.

They all saw that you were the first driver to accept your car and the first to leave the lot and get out onto the open road. They all watched as you navigated the landscape and hugged the curves with-out fear. Like a symphony in motion, because they saw how easy it looked for you, they followed your actions.

These drivers all appear to be confident, competent, and stable people. They all appear to have a strong sense of purpose. But there is a missing element. None of them know where they are going. They are all looking for direction in this adventure.

There is only one explanation for their actions. They can see something that you may have missed during this exercise in cour-age. They can all see that leadership has placed her mantle upon your shoulders and it now rests there without wavering. This team of cou-rageous, skillful drivers can see qualities they all admire.

They see courage. They see vision. They see that extraordinary attri-bute that led you to open the car door and take this uncharted quest.

They can see that you have a sense of destiny and they are willing to follow without question. They can see that you were born to lead.

Many Are Called

Many are called but few are chosen. Everyone receives a call at some point in her life. The problem is that many do not recognize the call when they receive it.

A call is when you have a knowing within you that you must do something for a specific reason. You feel compelled to do something. It becomes an almost overwhelming urge or hunger within you to act.

Once you accept the call, you must then decide how you are going to respond. Those who hesitate miss their opportunity to step into the realm of the chosen.

What is the difference between the called and the chosen? When a call for action comes, the called make one of the following choices: They stop and question the validity of the call, they make excuses for not responding, or they just ignore it.

The chosen respond differently. They hear the call and it is as if they've been waiting to hear it all their lives. The call fills them with energy and passion. The call becomes their focus and even if they can no longer hear it, they keep advancing. When they can no longer hear it, they go on a focused search until they regain direction. They become so ignited with passion that they will not rest until they reach their destination. The called then become transformed and driven to lead.

Have you ever had a burning or a desire for something that never seemed to subside? There is a burning that can only be extinguished by responding to destiny's call. Our response is what sets us apart. Our response is what makes us born to lead.

Everyone is invited but not everyone can handle the speed. It takes a special kind of courage to sit in the seat, step on the accelerator, and take the journey. Everyone is called but not everyone answers the call. But you answered. You acted. You are now in the driver's seat.

The Drive to Lead

Most of us drive. We use our cars to get to work, to run our errands and accomplish what needs to get done. Because of our way of life, we believe that driving is a necessity. But it's not—it's a privilege. In many countries women still are not allowed to drive. So if you are reading this and you live in the United States or Europe, you have access to this privilege just for the asking and the doing.

Leading and driving have much in common. Leading is a privilege. When someone selects you to lead, they honor you. When you elect to accept, you step into a place that can only be described as honorable. Without risk, there can be no honor. Honor is only gained when you take up a cause greater than yourself.

You have the honor and privilege of being in command of a mission. Your mission may be running your home, your office, or even a business. As a driver, you have the privilege of being in command of a vehicle. That vehicle could be the family van, a jeep, a luxury vehicle, or that car that keeps leaking oil. It doesn't matter because whatever it is, it belongs to you and you are responsible for it. The bottom line is that you are the commander of your mission and your mode of transportation.

A mission has critical elements that you must execute with precision for it to be successful. In driving, the vehicle must be handled with precision or the end result can be an accident or even death.

There are five principles that describe the operation of both driving and leadership. Those called to lead rise to their best when all principles, or facets, are operating together.

Leadership Facet 1: Activation/Ignition (Facing Challenges)

Activation is finding the ignition switch and looking for opportunities to experience something new and make changes. Activation also involves facing challenges or discovering new processes. Mission activates leadership. Leaders perform at their best when faced with a challenge. When confronted by a mission, those who are born to lead choose to *act*.

When a leader sees a need and then accepts the responsibility of meeting that need, activation occurs. When a driver gets into a vehicle, they start the car through the ignition system. Much like a rocket, the ignition process signals that the vehicle will soon be moving. Mission does the same for a leader.

Leadership Facet 2: Shifting into Gear/Direction (Inspiring Others to Share a Vision)

When a driver shifts a car into gear, they are the singular force deciding where the car will go. After a leader accepts a mission, they too become a force. This leadership force, unlike a car, is usually accompanied by a team. The leader decides on a course of action. Those who are born to lead believe that things do not have to stay the same. They believe they can make a difference and will pursue that goal with passion.

Like driving a car, they shift into gear and decide how best to execute their plans and operations. They decide if they need to advance or retreat from a position and how to gain an advantage over any threats. They then decide how best to move into the next facet of leadership. They also help others to see the possibilities of something new and exciting for the future.

Leadership Facet 3: Inspiration (Motivation)/Acceleration (Empowering Others to Act)

All drivers know where to locate the accelerator pedal in their cars.

It controls the speed of movement and how fast or how slowly they move towards their objective. It is the same with inspiration. True leaders inspire and empower others by creating an atmosphere of respect and shared vision. They foster mutual respect and help others to treat one another with dignity. This ability to work together with respect directly influences the mission.

They inspire and motivate their teams to move to the next level and take ownership of a mission. They do this by strengthening and empowering their team members to use their gifts. If this facet is not executed with precision and enthusiasm, the leader could lose their team and the mission could be lost.

Leadership Facet 4: Training and Development/Fueling (Showing Others How to Act)

Much like a car needs fuel in order to move, a team needs training. This also includes putting policies and procedures into action. Leaders understand that not all policies and procedures work, so they set in motion training scenarios to test them, ensuring that they are workable for mission success.

Leaders understand that training is a critical part of mission as much as drivers understand the need to fuel their vehicles. If a car does not receive fuel, then it will not move. If a team does not receive training, then they will fail to be mission-ready. Leaders set short-term goals and then model the desired behavior so that team members can see small victories while working towards the larger mission. This encourages team members to better see where they need to go and to work toward the larger group goals.

Leadership Facet 5: Rewards and Recognition/Maintenance (Rewarding and Encouraging Others)

As any good leader knows, recognition for a job well done is a critical element for keeping the team motivated. When a team reaches a remarkable goal, it is time for celebration! When leaders celebrate team members for a job well done, it infuses the team with hope and they are more willing to take ownership of the team mission.

If team members do not have ownership of a mission or they feel unappreciated, then they will lack the passion to work toward goals. Having a "shared heart" is essential to the success of any mission. In other words, people must feel important if they are to function at their best.

If a driver does not perform regular maintenance on their vehicle, engine failure could result. The care and feeding of a team is much like the care and feeding of a car. Both ensure that the car and team stay ready to meet challenges.

As you read through this book, you will see the five leadership facets woven throughout the fabric of each leadership style. The end result will be the same but each journey will display the colors and textures of the leadership style.

Where Do We Go from Here?

It still may not be easy to see how these leadership facets impact your life. Right now, you may still believe that you are not called to be a leader. But the fact is that every person who exists is called into some sort of leadership position. That includes you.

To assist you in seeing how these facets look when operating in your life, take the Leadership Style Inventory. It is a simple instrument which will help you discover your leadership style and how to use it. It's like trying on a new dress. Just try and see how it fits. It won't hurt, but it could be one of the most fabulous things you ever experience. It is also helpful to know who you are before you fully operate in your style.

Isn't it exciting to know that God did not forget you when He passed out the leadership gifts? If you don't feel the excitement yet, you will. Watching God's power flow through you to influence the lives of others is nothing short of miraculous. Excitement is a natural result of that experience.

As you begin this journey, remember that it is an honor to lead others, and those who are lost are waiting for you to show them the way to destiny. Each person you touch is called to lead, and God has chosen you to help with this mission. So let's get started!

2

The Leadership Style Inventory

If you don't know who you are, you will
never know what belongs to you!

Did you know that identity is a critical facet of life? Everything around you shouts its identity to the world. If you just stop and listen, you can hear the birds singing, the wind blowing, the dogs barking, the sun shining, and the stars twinkling. These sounds and sights let you know that these things are players on the world's stage and it's their time to sing, blow, bark, shine, and twinkle. Everything in them displays their identity. It is the same with you.

You are a woman and the essence of your femininity is present with every breath you take and every move you make. And so it is with your leadership style. You have a style that announces your presence and identity to others. Others can see it in something as simple as the way you wave your hands when you talk or the way you thump on your desk with your pen while thinking. It is a part of who you are and you cannot help but announce it to the world, much like the birds, the wind, that barking dog, the sun, and the stars.

Others may not like your style but once you are comfortable with your own beauty and power, that won't matter. It won't matter because once you accept it you will discover a new wave of freedom. This freedom can catapult you to success, but not accepting it can lead to heartache. The heartache comes when you allow others to stop the flow of your style.

No one else is like you. No one can do what you do the way that you do it. You are just that awesome and unique!

Do Men and Women Lead Differently?

I've heard people say that women lead differently than men. While this could be true, we will see that leadership is not a gender-based quality. I do believe that God placed the same gifts in both men and women. The gifts only look different when painted with gender.

Let's explore this for a moment. Your leadership style is like a T-shirt. Both men and women can wear T-shirts. But the shirt looks different depending on who's wearing it! It may not change in fabric, texture, or color, but the context gives it a different shape or style.

For example, a man decides to wear a blue T-shirt to work on his car. He soils it with oil and black engine grease. It doesn't bother him that he ruined his new shirt. He purchased it to wear for outdoor work like this. To him, it is just a good work shirt and it served his purpose. The oil and grease did not hinder the process. They are just the physical reminders of how he operates.

A woman purchases and then wears the same style shirt with her favorite pair of jeans. She puts on her makeup and styles her hair. She then visits friends and goes shopping. The shirt remains clean. She wears it all day and it still looks clean by day's end. She purchased the shirt to function as an active part of her wardrobe. The shirt still served a purpose and remained clean.

Both worked in their T-shirts. The only thing that changed was the activity of the person wearing the shirt. One wore the shirt as a work tool, the other as a part of an active lifestyle. And so it is with leadership. The mission may be different but the facets of leadership are the same no matter who is leading.

The Leadership Style Inventory

On the following pages, you will take the Leadership Style Inventory. Once you discover your style, you can gain more insight on how to more effectively operate in your role as a leader. It will also help you discover how to deal with challenging people and situations. As you discover the wonderful details of feminine leadership, you will also discover that you truly are born to lead. Learning your style also frees you to be comfortable with just being you!

Read each statement and circle the letter beside the one that sounds most like you.

1. **Which of the following statements best describes your focus when working with a team?**
   A. Build. I can build something no one else can.
   B. Plan. I can develop the plan to accomplish the mission.
   C. Execute. I can do that. Just give me the freedom to do what I do.
   D. Create. I can see a new way of doing things.
   E. Cooperate. I know who to partner with to get the job done.
   F. Risk. I can cut through red tape and get us where we need to go.

2. **In which of the following ways do you engage others in the process when leading a team?**
   A. You share what you know so everyone will know what you know.
   B. You plan what you'll do so others have direction.

   C. You act on what you know and encourage others to follow.

   D. You show others how to creatively use their gifts to achieve the mission.

   E. You encourage others to accept and work with others.

   F. You allow others to shine because when the team shines, you shine.

3. Which of the following statements best describes your core position when it comes to working with others?

   A. Accomplish the mission...yesterday.

   B. Overtake the details or they will take over you.

   C. Show me the mission and I'll overcome the challenges.

   D. Let's try something different. It might just work.

   E. A true leader allows others to lead too.

   F. A true leader has no problem taking risks. It comes with the territory.

4. You want to work with others who...

   A. are open to change and don't mind working hard to accomplish a task.

   B. are strategic in their thinking and open to planning each step of the process.

   C. are precise in their execution and know how to improvise if needed.

   D. are resourceful and creative in their problem-solving.

   E. work willingly with others and believe in strength in unity.

   F. are risk-takers and love the recognition that comes with victory.

5. Which of the following best describes your attitude when sharing your vision?

   A. No change, no movement.

B. No plan, no success.

C. No flexibility, no triumph.

D. No originality, no ownership.

E. No collaboration, no unity.

F. No glorious cause, no victory.

6. **What is the best way to help your team members see your vision as a leader?**

A. Show them areas where you need something new and different done.

B. Show them how you believe they fit in with your plan.

C. Show them the skills you need for each facet so they can see the best place for themselves.

D. Show them areas where they can use creative problem-solving.

E. Show them areas where you need to bring in outside assistance.

F. Show them areas where your team could gain recognition.

7. **How do you help others take ownership of a mission or project?**

A. You help them see where a new way of doing things is needed and then allow them to assist you in implementing the changes.

B. You lay out the plan and allow them to give feedback before you finalize the plan.

C. You allow them to see where they fit and then oversee or supervise that particular area of the mission.

D. You give them the mission details and ask how they would do things differently from what you have planned.

E. You ask them if and how to best use outside resources and allow them to coordinate that portion of the mission.

F. You show them the mission and ask if they see any missing parts. If they do, allow them to close the gaps.

8. **How do you build trust in your team?**

A. You work with alongside your team and allow them to see that no task is too lowly or too small for you to perform.

B. You allow them to see the plan and see how they fit into the mission.

C. You give them small tasks so they gain small victories which lead to larger tasks and greater victories.

D. You allow them to take the lead, test new methods, and evaluate them without judgment or negative repercussions.

E. You become transparent and allow them to see that without them the mission will fail. You then allow them to help with decision-making and team leadership.

F. You give them space to make decisions that impact team operations while working closely with them to ensure that those decisions best benefit the team.

9. **How do you react when you do not agree with an established policy?**

A. Lobby until you are heard.

B. Develop a plan and capture data to support your objections before presenting them.

C. Listen and share your opinion to see if others share your views. Then you work with others to develop plans to present to decision-makers.

D. Create a new policy that will still meet the needs of the organization while taking into account the needs of the team.

E. Research to see what's being done in other organizations and then work with others to make changes.

F. Schedule meetings to share your opinions and take the lead in making what you see as necessary changes.

10. **Which of the following statements best describes how you promote growth within the ranks of your team?**

A. You allow them to take on projects to upgrade or change outdated policies.

B. You allow them to develop plans for future projects and present their ideas.

C. You allow them to take the lead on projects and mentor more inexperienced team members.

D. You allow them to develop new projects, investigate new methods, and test new materials that will help to accomplish the mission.

E. You encourage them to attend conferences and trainings outside your organization to help strengthen outside relationships.

F. You allow them to take the lead in publicizing and marketing the team. This may mean serving as a spokesperson or a similar function.

11. **When someone openly challenges you as a leader, you...**

A. do not stop working on the mission and wait to deal with the situation until everything is finished.

B. immediately take note of the incident. You write up a report to take action later.

C. stop everything. You confront the person and deal with the infraction immediately.

D. ignore it. Perhaps the person is having a bad day.

E. talk to the group as a whole about the importance of working together as a team, hoping the person will get the message and you will not have to single her out.

F. confront and chastise the person on the spot. Immediate
    dishonor requires immediate attention.

12. **Which of the following statements/actions best describes how
    you respond when something goes wrong with a mission?**

A. Let's redo it. We will work without stopping until we find
    out what went wrong.

B. We must have missed something in the planning. Let's find
    it.

C. Show me the crisis and I'll show you the best way to solve
    it.

D. We could do things differently since the way we did them
    did not work.

E. Let's see what others have done. We may need some
    outside assistance.

F. If this didn't work, we need to form new teams and start
    over. I'll lead the way.

Scores

If you scored more A's, you operate as an *Activist Leader.*
If you scored more B's, you operate as a *Strategic Leader.*
If you scored more C's, you operate as a *Tactical Leader.*
If you scored more D's, you operate as a *Creative Leader.*
If you scored more E's, you operate as a *Collaborative Leader.*
If you scored more F's, you operate as a *Dramatic Leader.*

Every person has a dominant leadership style. This is the way you
would lead most of the time. That can change depending upon the
mission, the group you are leading, and even what is happening in
your life at the time you are leading. All these factors play an important role in how you see yourself as a leader.

God created you with a leadership style that will help you lead
with excellence and bring out the best in others, but you must first

embrace it and learn to walk in it. Remember that leadership is like a mantle or cape that drapes around your shoulders. It fits you perfectly. There is nothing missing when it comes to your leadership style… nothing but acceptance. This is where we sometimes make mistakes. We do not believe that we are leaders because we make mistakes.

Here's a news flash! Leaders can and do make mistakes. But good leaders first admit they made a mistake. They also have a desire to learn from those mistakes and use them to identify strengths and recognize their areas of challenge. They learn to operate with power in their areas of strength and they learn to allow others who are gifted in their areas of challenge to walk beside them to enhance and expand their leadership scope.

After taking the Leadership Style Inventory, you have that same opportunity. You can embrace and walk freely in the beauty and power of your leadership style and understand you will need the help of others in order to walk in excellence while leading. Depending on others is not a weakness. It is an open display of strength. It's like fishing. You can catch one fish at a time with a pole but if you use a net, you can catch many fish.

Walking alone allows you to catch or impact just one person at a time. But when you train a team and allow them to discover and embrace their individual leadership styles, you form a network where many will be served. You become a force to be reckoned with. You become unstoppable. You become a leader who walks without fear or excuse. You send the enemy running for cover because you will not be stopped from attaining your goals.

It's a wonder that the enemy doesn't wise up and just leave us alone. I, for one do not enjoy fighting with other women. Can you imagine what would happen if we came together as leaders to fight him? Once we embrace the obvious fact that God created us to lead, we can accomplish anything…including making the enemy run for cover!

You are changing every day into someone more beautiful than you know and more powerful than you can imagine. God is in control of your journey and He is calling you to join Him as He places this leadership mantle upon your lovely shoulders.

So, unstoppable woman, it's time to walk in the beauty and power of your leadership birthright. Your journey is just beginning!

The Choice Is Yours

"Hey, you can't do that! That's not allowed. You can't do that 'cause it's against the rules," he said as he picked up my boulder.

"What rules? I didn't hear you say anything about that before." I shouted as I snatched my favorite blue and yellow boulder from his hands. This was a stand-off and I was not going to lose. The three other boys got to their feet as we moved toward one another. We were so close that I could feel his breath on my face, but I was unafraid. I clutched my boulder and my bag of marbles. I could feel the blood rush to my head and a wave of fear tried to overtake me.

"You're out. You don't follow the rules. We don't want you here anymore. Every time you come, you start trouble." The other boys nodded in agreement. Where was my help? Where was my support? Where was the chorus of feminine voices I needed to defend me and my position? You guessed it. They were in the house playing with dolls.

I felt as if my stomach was about to throw its contents on the chalk circle that surrounded the marble game. I could feel the sting of tears trying to burst through my resolve and force themselves into the corners of my eyes. I wanted to cry and then tell them off but I couldn't utter a word. I was humiliated as they stood there laughing. I couldn't fight them off.

The testosterone wall was now up, and these boys had drawn new boundaries that I could not cross. They changed the rules every time I gained a victory. I knew that even if I protested, they would not be able to hear my voice. So I picked up my straw purse, which had once been filled with marbles, and walked home.

Playing marbles was one my favorite childhood activities. I played marbles with the boys and fought with the best of them. At the same time, I loved wearing dresses. I wanted to wear my dresses but I also wanted to do things the boys did. So I decided that I would still wear dresses when I went out to play but I had an extra added feature. I wore shorts under my dresses. I also needed something to carry my marbles in so I also took my purse and boldly entered the marble arena. Inside my purse was my white washcloth. I needed the cloth to place on the ground so I would not scar up my knees when I shot.

Looking back, I still remember the surprised expressions on the boys' faces when I came to the shoot. Their whispers and laughs did not deter me. I was the only girl and the only African American present, but that did not bother me. I wanted to compete and I could see that competition was the essence of their world. I wanted to be a part of it. I also wanted the freedom I saw when they played together.

At first, the boys did not take me seriously. They humored me by teaching me their games and told me that since I was just a girl that I would never be as good as they were. They soon learned that it really did not matter what you wore or what gender you were as long as you really wanted to win. I won marble games wearing my dresses and with my purse on my arm. Instead of buying doll clothes with my extra money, I bought guns and ammunition. I especially loved the cap pistols and water guns. I always carried a weapon and some lipstick (samples from Avon) in my purse when I went out to play.

Being with boys was great fun until they changed the rules in the middle of a game. Of course, I pointed out the unfairness to no avail. When they ignored my protests, I threw my marbles in my little purse and went home.

When I talked to my mother about it, she told me that I had

no business playing with boys and that losing was the result of that choice. So I swallowed my disappointment and tried to reenter the world of girls. With a forced smile, I played with my dolls. I liked the dolls that I could change into stylish outfits. Baby dolls would not do, especially since I had real babies living in the house with me. I was the chief diaper changer and bottle washer.

Growing up as the first of seven children was not easy. My father wanted sons but God had other plans. He gave him a line of five girls before the two boys came along. As the firstborn, I learned to watch sports with him. I also played cards with him. And since he was a chef, he even taught me to cook. Daddy and I had great conversations and I learned about the world of men from him. It was great fun, especially since he always seemed to have a freedom I did not understand.

He told me stories about his time in the military. I would envision how it felt being in the military and even told him that I wanted to become a soldier. While he didn't mind my listening to his stories, he did not want any of his daughters to serve in the military. This, he said, was for men.

It was difficult for me to grasp that I could not play marbles and still remain feminine. I loved wearing dresses. I loved playing with an occasional doll, but there was nothing like the thrill of swinging from a tree with a machine gun in hand. There was nothing in my feminine world that could compare with shooting marbles. I lived for the thrill of the hunt and the winning of the game. My parents didn't understand that I was not the quiet little female type and demanded that I conform. I soon learned that in order to emotionally survive, I would need to assimilate and become what the world called *ladylike* and completely feminine.

What we learn as children about who we are or who we are supposed to be greatly influences how we see ourselves as adults. I did not realize at that stage of my life that the Lord created each person different and beautifully unique.

We stand at the doors of life and our enemy will do everything in his power to discourage and oppress us so that we will not lead and encourage other leaders. If he convinces us that we should not be leading, he wins. If he convinces us to stop and sit on the sidelines of life, he wins. If he convinces us that we should not teach other women how to lead, he wins.

So what are you going to do about it? Will you sit there and do nothing or will you stand and fight? The choice is yours.

3

The Activist Leader

Leading without considering people is a
failed mission from the beginning!

If you scored more A's on the Leadership Style Inventory, you operate in the Activist leadership style. Words that describe you are...

- advocate
- forward looking and thinking
- futuristic
- innovative
- ahead of your time

You have no problem with the word *vision* because you can see what others seem to miss. You have a gift for helping others work and move together toward a common goal. You help your team members see the vision and then prepare them to persevere and move forward together as a team.

Whenever the need for a project appears, you like being in the midst of things. You are the one who rolls up her sleeves and immediately goes to work. You and procrastination cannot coexist. You are a savvy project manager and you love the feeling of accomplishment. Loose ends do not agree with your spirit and you wish others could see and feel the joy of a task completed. You can see the end result and you know instinctively how something should look when it is completed. It comes with the territory of being a visionary Activist Leader.

Because you love completion, one of your pet peeves is hearing complaints. Whenever work needs to be done, you don't hesitate but start before anyone else. Some team members have no problem with standing around and talking and complaining about what is to be done, but not you. "Just get the work done, and we can all go home," is your leadership theme.

Everyone agrees that you are a burst of energy. You work from sunup to sundown, many times without taking a break. While completing a project is important, is also important to take care of yourself so you can continue doing what you do. Stop and do something relaxing where work in not the main focus. If you don't have a hobby, develop one. As an Activist, you must develop some balance. So take a deep breath and, every once in a while, try to enjoy the journey.

Activist Leadership Strengths

As an Activist leader, you have boundless energy. Couple this energy with your focus and ability to ignore distractions, and you've got an incredible strength! You openly share knowledge and information with team members because you understand that without knowledge people and the vision they carry cannot thrive. Your team members enjoy working with you because you share information so openly.

You keep everyone informed of new policies and procedures and help them to navigate the fierce waters of corporate politics. Although you are aware of how important politics can be, you have little interest in it, keeping your team members mindful of the mission.

You are an enlightened leader who has no problem accepting what others deem to be an impossible task. You shine when a group needs to follow a new direction or a new mission needs implementation. You thrive and have a positive, powerful impact on organizational climate when newness fills the air. You run to meet challenges and because of your vision, your team willingly follows.

You are a quick study and because you are a visionary, you can see the end of mission without detailed instructions. You place the puzzle pieces together and quickly assign team members to areas where they can best use their gifts. You allow team members autonomy in developing new ways to do old tasks and watch as skin and muscle appear on the dry bones of the project. You then assign someone to take notes and develop new manuals to serve as guides for future project leaders.

You have the unique ability to pick up projects others thought dead and resurrect them because you are able to see the embers still glowing from creation's fire. You are an expert at reviving them. Because you are a visionary, you can see details left undone and discover jewels left undiscovered.

There are times when you appear to be intrusive. When you want to know something, you ask. If you don't feel that you can ask, you will investigate. You will turn over every rock and move every mountain in order to do a thorough job of finding information. Others quickly learn that they might as well tell you what you want to know because you will find out what you want regardless of how they treat you.

Because you are forward thinking, when faced with a task you prepare by working through multiple scenarios. By doing this, you prepare for what others call the unexpected because you want to be able to handle any surprises.

Even if you take on a challenge and are unsuccessful, you do not believe that failing makes you a failure. You believe that failing in one area means that you are closer to a solution in another. In other words, you investigate and create until the situation changes. If the changes are not apparent, then you create scenarios to replay what you did and make corrections. For you, there is always a solution to a problem and it will not remain hidden for long.

When given a job, you are always focused on doing what is necessary to get that job done. Mission is your middle name and completing that mission is your theme. Everyone who works with you knows it.

You are the first to serve as an advocate when one of your team members faces challenges. You work tirelessly to ensure that policies and procedures are fair. If you discover a policy that hinders your mission, you have no problem confronting decision makers to have the policies changed. One might say that you even "get on people's nerves" because you can be relentless when you believe something is unfair. Your team members love it when they see this facet of your leadership style in action. The team and the mission are direct beneficiaries of this powerful facet of your leadership style.

You have no problem writing letters, attending public forums, using your personal resources, or seeking professional assistance in order to see a policy changed. You'll do whatever it takes because in your eyes, injustice to your team cannot coexist with your mission.

Miriam

She walked through the waters and lived!

> Then Miriam the prophet, Aaron's sister, took a tambourine and led all the women as they played their tambourines and danced (Exodus 15:20).

Imagine standing in the desert and watching as a pillar of fire blocks the path of a bloodthirsty army. Their sole mission is to destroy you and your people. The heated atmosphere causes you to tremble because there is no apparent way of escape. The Red Sea now stands in front of you. The pillar of fire—not to mention the army—stops you from going back the way you came.

The jagged rocks lining the shore serve as silent sentinels, warning those who try to cross the mighty waters. They send you taunting mental messages, reminding you that your fate may be to drown in the sea's waves. It reminds you that you are merely human and today can only be saved by the divine.

As hope frees you from his embrace, you feel the wind change. It caresses your face with warm, silent fingertips as if to tell you that no matter what the situation looks like, things are going to be fine. As the wind dances through your hair, it whirls, twirls, and increases with such speed and force that it nearly knocks you off your feet. You gasp for breath as it forms a current so strong that it slices the sea waters like a hot knife cutting through butter.

To your surprise, it then creates a pathway exposing dry ground on the sea floor. Can this be true? The same wind that nearly knocked you off your feet has suddenly made a pathway large enough for you and all you know to cross to an unknown land.

Now, see yourself stepping onto the dry ground, surrounded by transparent walls of water. This journey's unique events have made you feel like a child. You realize that all the happenings are not man-made and there is Someone other than man leading and protecting you. There can be no other explanation. You know that there is no way that man could have made the laughing waves and Pharaoh's army stand still. You also realize that the only way you and your people can go is forward.

Today there is no room for fear. Today is a day for the sure-footed. You and your loved ones have tripped over the stones of self-doubt and slavery and allowed fear to rule you for over 400 years. There are few words that can describe the majestic beauty of this moment. You only know that you must move forward. Something is drawing your energy into the sea. Something is pulling you forward. With each step, you must summon every ounce of physical strength locked within your muscles to propel your legs and feet forward. You also understand that you are recording history with each step. You can sense that this is a time for celebration so you do what comes natural to you. You lead. You lead all the way to the land promised to you and your people by God.

Like you, your sister Miriam assessed her situation and led her family and her people through certain danger. She had to exercise her faith in such a new way, changing her and all those connected to her. She had to capture courage when he tried to make his escape. She had to summon power when he buried himself in desert sands. She had to drown fear in the Rea Sea. Like you and other Activist leaders do every day, she led as she taught. In other words…she walked her talk.

Miriam helped to lead her people across the Red Sea and into the Promised Land. Her bravery and the ability to see a new future propelled her to move with purpose and step into her destiny as a powerful visionary called to lead by the Most High!

Activist Leadership Style Challenges

Because you enjoy projects and programs, there are times when you may appear to be unfeeling when it comes to people. You forge ahead when it comes to work and after you give out information, you want your team to move without further instruction or direction. Giving detailed directions is usually not one of your strengths. Once you give information on a project, you expect others to see where they fit into the process. In other words, you expect them to catch the vision.

You sometimes forget that you carry the vision and can see all aspects of the picture. You see the entire portrait and because of your anxiousness to complete the mission, you may leave some facets of it left unshared. Take time to write it down and share the complete vision with your team. Since you are so great at sharing information, this will not be difficult for you.

Although it may not fit in with your usual way of operating, it will benefit you to write your plans down and give out not only project information but also individual instructions to team members. This will alleviate confusion and allow team members to operate more effectively in their assigned areas of responsibility because they will no longer be "blind" while working.

You are often misjudged. Because of your boundless energy, you may appear to be brassy and even borderline bossy to others. People may believe that you do not care for your team. They would be wrong. Taking care of your team is your Achilles heel. There are times when you cross boundaries and become too closely involved in the personal lives of your team. This could lead to challenges in leading since you may place the personal needs of an individual before the needs and goals of the team.

As an activist leader, it is important to respect boundaries. Developing deep, personal friendships with team members can become sticky, possibly placing the team and mission in danger of failure. You could then fall into leading by the strength of your emotions instead of in the power of your Activist leadership style.

You are like a human tornado when it comes to work. You hate complaining and will remove yourself from the presence of complainers. You believe that once a job is assigned, then it's time to go to work. Work is what keeps you sharp. Your gift of vision is what gets the work done. These two factors are inseparable tools in your leadership toolbox.

Others may not share the fire of your vision, and this could cause you some stress. Accepting that others may not work at your pace or have your inner compass for direction will help relieve your stress. It's okay to relax a bit until others catch up with you. Some of your team members may not ever see what you see. Just help them to see how they fit into the vision by accepting them and helping them to use their gifts where they are.

You meet your most difficult leadership challenges when leading more experienced team members. They may need more structure and focus than you want to give. In order to lead these team members, you must not allow their behavior or judgmental attitudes to intimidate you. They may be more experienced and educated, but remember that they still need leadership.

You are the leader and these experienced warriors will test you to see if you will stand your ground. If you pass the test, then they will come alongside you and hold up your arms as you lead. They need to see your strength of character and commitment to the process since they may not see the experience. Once this happens, you can allow these seasoned members to serve as assistants in helping other team members achieve success!

The Activist Leader and the Five Leadership Facets

Leadership Facet 1: Activation/Ignition

For you, completing a mission is like driving a jeep. You take the rough terrain of a mission and make it look easy. You realize that the team comes before the mission. Without the team, there can be no mission. You focus on working as one unit and not so much on individual progress. This is an area where you can use those more experienced team members to fill in the blanks for you. You assign them to watch over less experienced members and assist them with tasks when necessary. Connections made during these times benefit not only those directly involved but the entire team. This is team cohesion at its best.

You do not play favorites and find the practice offensive and disruptive. You've seen far too many teams disintegrate because of favoritism. It creates division and misunderstanding and erodes team confidence. Your job as a leader is to ensure that each team member performs the tasks for which they have been trained to the best of their ability. When favoritism rears its ugly head, it stops productivity. And you know favoritism can eat away at the foundation of hard work and morale like cancer.

Leadership Facet 2: Shifting into Gear/Direction

As an activist leader, when you shift your jeep into gear it's usually full throttle. You want things done...yesterday! Because you want things completed, you may miss the best way to get things done. Be cautious about taking the path of least resistance in order to complete a task. The easiest way may not always be the best way to get the job done well.

Stop and take a deep breath. Study your map before beginning the journey. The direct road may not be the best road. Check to make sure that what you want is still available. There may be construction or the road may be closed. Check the weather so you can have all the proper equipment. Just because something looks easy doesn't mean that it will be easy. There may be traps, pits of quicksand, or other unseen obstacles. You have to be prepared.

It also helps to keep you dependent on your circle of counsel. Engage your team. Take a look around and see who always talks about the weather. Listen and figure out who has a passion for map reading. Someone on your team enjoys checking road conditions and another team member takes joy in ensuring that you have the proper emergency equipment.

Remember, there is safety in a multitude of counsel and you have no problem seeking help should you need it.

Leadership Facet 3: Inspiration (Motivation)/Acceleration

Lead by example is the motto of the activist leader. To inspire others, you are the first to jump in and work when it comes to mission. No job is beneath you. Even if you are leading a ditch-digging job, you will be the first to get your hands dirty and be lead ditch-digger. You inspire your team members by standing with them. As an activist leader, you understand that in order to accelerate your vehicle, you must lead by example. This inspires your team to move. But they still need clear direction.

It doesn't take much to motivate them if they can see the purpose of a mission. When they ask questions, it is usually for a good reason. Don't get offended. Although you freely share information, it is not always clear. If things are unclear, share as only an activist leader can do and let them know what you know.

Leadership Facet 4: Training and Development/Fueling

As an activist leader, you may need some assistance in this area because you don't want to stop and refuel. You sometimes forget that your jeep will stop mid-mission if you do not take time to refuel. You love working until the job gets done even if you don't have the tools or people in place. Your main focus is completion. Completion can come at an exorbitant cost if you do not stop and refuel.

Training your team to do a job is one thing, but checking to ensure that they remember the skills they learned is quite another. Your jeep needs fuel and does not need operation information imparted by you. It is a piece of equipment. It does exactly what you tell it to do as long as you keep up the maintenance. People are much more complex. Watch and allow team members to demonstrate their skills by having them perform tasks during times when no emergency exists.

Evaluate your team members to identify which ones have strengths in training and allow them to assist you. Your team needs training and you will be able to see how some of your other team members grasp the vision. You are called to train and equip other leaders so train, equip, and release them into their destiny by allowing them to thrive. Watch as the vision takes shape!

Leadership Facet 5: Rewards and Recognition/Maintenance

As an activist leader, you understand that rewarding others is a significant facet of mission success. You also understand that recognition is a form of motivation that can move a team to complete a mission. Because of your love for completing things, this speaks to you. You make sure that recognition is one of the key elements in your leadership model.

If there are no policies in place in your organization for recognizing team members, you develop them. You have no problem with even spending your own money and accessing your resources to make it happen. You understand that recognition is like an oil change for a vehicle. If the oil is dirty it makes the car sluggish and impacts gas mileage. You do not intend to allow your vehicle to stall or to operate below par. You recognize team members with joy!

Look Up!

There is nothing more powerful than an Activist leader who understands that when things look down, she needs to look up. She understands that in order to be a successful leader, she must sometimes look outside herself to help find answers to difficult questions and to help her face challenges. When an Activist leader is down and looks up, she is at her leadership best. So, when you need help, lift your head. When you need clarity, lift your eyes. When you need counsel, open your ears then lift your arms and hands upward and behold…the miraculous!

Lucy Stone (1818-1893)

Her legacy was identity.

"Lucy Stone!" It was a like a dream. When they called her name, even she could hardly believe it. But it was true. She had earned her college degree. All her years of study had earned her both a degree and the distinction of being the class valedictorian. Not bad for a girl who used to weave fabric, can fruits, and sew piecework at the local shoe factory. Now she could add "the first woman college graduate in America" to her credentials.

She remembered the days when she and her eight siblings tended the cows and worked hard to support the family. There had been some hard days but for the most part, she remembered that her father drank heavily and ruled the household with an iron fist. Although they had a steady but modest income from selling cheese, Hannah, her mother, did not have access to the family funds.

Lucy cringed every time she heard Hannah beg her father for money to buy clothing and other family necessities. When he refused, Hannah would wait until her husband fell asleep after one of his drinking binges and then steal coins from his purse.

I will not live this way when I leave here. I will not allow a man to dictate if I can clothe and feed my children, Lucy thought almost aloud. It angered her whenever she thought of the way her mother had to run her household and was determined that her life would be different. And if she had anything to do with it, it would be different for other women as well. Although she had already had a teaching career, a degree would enable her to earn more money.

As she walked up to the platform to take her degree in her hands, she walked into history. This activist leader would not only be the first woman to earn a college degree in America, she would also go on to organize the first national convention for women's rights. For over twenty years she edited the *Woman's Journal*, a weekly magazine which targeted the suffrage movement. She also wrote many articles for the publication. Because of her passion for the rights of others, she also became an outspoken opponent of slavery. But her heart was for women, regardless of their ethnicity, and what they experienced.

"In education, in marriage, in religion, in everything, disappointment is the lot of women. It shall be the business of my life to deepen that disappointment in every woman's heart until she bows down to it no longer," she said. These words still echo through history's halls and into the workplace and homes of even today's women around the world.

Lucy passed the editorial baton for the *Woman's Journal* on to her daughter, Alice Stone Blackwell, who then served as the editor for 35 years. Lucy's last words to her daughter were, "Make the world better."

She lived her life serving others and working for a cause greater than herself. Like you, this activist leader changed the course of history while changing the lives of those around her. She lived to serve others and to see people, regardless of creed, color, or gender, walk in purpose!

Activist Leadership Tips

Don't let others change you.

Because of your energy, others can misunderstand your motives. They may believe that you are trying to gain an unfair advantage in a given situation. They may also believe that you are trying to steal all the limelight from others. Nothing could be further from the truth.

What they don't know is that the limelight is not what you seek. You don't need it. You do not work for attention. You work because you love the feeling of accomplishment and seeing something come together. You also enjoy watching others grow in character as they learn new skills. Standing on stage is not your goal, although leadership sometimes demands it. You prefer working behind the scenes.

As a mission-focused activist leader, you set the pace for your team. So continue to lead in the beauty of your style and others will soon see the real you at work. Continue to set the pace and be yourself. Remember, no one has the gifts and personality God gave you. So enjoy being you!

Take a break.

It's okay to take a break. Projects take on a life of their own and you can either collapse under the pressure or take charge! In other words, you have to take control over the project and how and when you execute it. That means you are in charge. Break projects into small portions and allow your team to assist you. This is why it is critical that you understand the strengths of each team member so that when you need help with specific tasks, you know whom to assign.

It's okay to stop and enjoy your life, even when there are things that need to be done. The dishes will still be there after your break. That report will still be waiting for you. The project will still be there, especially if you delegate. Things will get done. There are people who need your hugs and attention. Don't let work stifle your relationships.

The need for hugs will pass if you pass on the moments they are standing there waiting. Children grow up and leave. Friends will wait just so long. You don't want to find your arms aching for their hugs just because you chose a project over those moments. Stop and take a break!

Don't take on more than you can realistically handle.

Many times, as a mission-focused activist leader, you will take on more projects than you can handle. You then become overwhelmed. This feeling of being overwhelmed leads to anger, frustration, and isolation. You may then believe that you are failing at life. Remember, failing doesn't mean that you are a failure. When you start feeling this way, it's time to get help.

One main concern for an activist leader is actually accepting help when it arrives. There are times when you have to let your guard down and receive help. It's okay to delegate. It's okay to allow someone else to make the hard decisions. It is not a negative reflection on your leadership abilities. Quite the contrary, because delegation is a critical ingredient to helping others become strong leaders.

Do not fall into the trap of thinking that you have to be everything to everyone! You are a powerful woman with fabulous abilities. Just make sure you rid your life of projects that you really don't want to do. Find an intern. Colleges have intern placement offices that can help. Outsource the work to a protégé. There are many women in need of job training and who will welcome the opportunity to serve as your assistant. There is always someone who would be delighted to do the work.

As an activist leader, you can work smart and not hard to get the job done. Don't let the joy stealers take away your creativity, knowledge, or power. Remember that you are an asset and you bring gifts to share with others. So open those gifts and allow your light to shine brightly as you lead others.

Joan Ganz Cooney

She put children out in the street; Sesame Street that is!

"I wish I could tell you that the Children's Television Workshop and Sesame Street were thanks to my genius, but it really was a lucky break," said this modern-day heroine of educational television. But it's what activist leader Joan Ganz Cooney did with that break that makes her so phenomenal.

In the mid-1960s, Cooney noticed that children seemed to remember the jingles and fast-paced-repetition of television commercials. Because of this, she sensed that television could play a pivotal role in educating children. She wanted to use the multi-segment template for her educational curriculum. This sparked her idea to create the Children's Television Network.

"There is a young and impressionable mind out there that is hungry for information. It has latched on to an electronic tube as its main source of nourishment," said Cooney. She intended to make sure that as long as children were going to be watching television, they would also be learning something of value.

She envisioned a show that would teach math and reading in an hour-long format. It would be patterned after adult shows like *Rowan and Martin's Laugh-In*, which consisted of short, funny segments that captured the audience's attention and then quickly moved on. Cooney's hunch was right and the Children's Television Network launched in 1969.

Although her boss and other television executives were skeptical, activist leader Cooney forged ahead with her idea and consulted educators who supported her philosophy. She also managed to get financial support from the Carnegie Foundation and the US Commissioner of Education. One year and eight million dollars later, she silenced her critics when Sesame Street hit the television airwaves.

"Cherishing children is the mark of a civilized society," Cooney said. And she set out to prove that our nation did, in fact, cherish children when she created the Children's Television Network. Your activist leader sister not only created a program where numbers, letters, and puppets were the stars, but she also allowed children to see diversity at work. Her human characters displayed a microcosm of America's diverse population. Children saw Asian, Hispanic, white, and African American people working together in the Sesame Street neighborhood.

Today, almost four decades and over four thousand episodes later, the Children's Television Network, now called Sesame Workshop, has won numerous awards. *Sesame Street*, its flagship program, is considered a national treasure. Children still watch Big Bird and company to learn their ABCs and 123s.

In 1995, Cooney won the Presidential Medal of Freedom for her work. As an activist leader driven by a passion for children, she did not take *no* for an answer. She found the support and funding to create the magic of Sesame Street!

Dancing with the Right Partner

> For the Lord is the Spirit, and wherever the Spirit of the
> Lord is, there is freedom (2 Corinthians 3:17).

Freedom looks and feels different to each individual. As an activist leader, you must have a clear understanding of not only freedom but also what it means to be in bondage. You must be clear because if you dance with freedom, so will your team. If you dance with bondage, so will your team. You can hinder or enhance your team's performance by choosing the right dance partner.

So what does freedom look like to you? What does it feel like to you? How do you know when you have freedom in your life? Which do you believe is more powerful, freedom or bondage? Let's take a look at both.

Bondage is powerful. When it holds us, we feel powerless, hopeless, faithless, and oppressed. It can hold us in such captivity that there are times when we cannot even see a way of escape. We see only what our spiritual cataracts allow us to see.

We grow accustomed to operating within the scope of self-imposed limitations and never attempt to break free. Our minds operate in a diseased state, making us stand in the buffet line of oppression and await our fill of depression-laced consumables.

This reminds of me of a television program I saw some time ago. Someone discovered an elephant that had been held captive in a ten-foot-square enclosure for most of its life. From the time it was a just a baby, it had lived in this tiny space. Of course when he was young, the space was okay. But when the elephant began to grow, the space was not only a physically limiting environment but it impacted the elephant emotionally. The larger he became, the more he was aware of his captivity.

We can imagine that when the elephant was young, he tried to escape but the brick walls stopped him. He moved his body against the prison walls and tried without success to make them fall. He did this for years and the wall remained. His rebellious bumping soon became a pathetic rocking. He understood the limits of his prison and although there was some small part of him that resisted, his massive body still hit the walls of his prison. The walls then became a part of not only his physical prison, but they caused the elephant to believe that they would be a permanent fixture in his life.

When rescuers finally released him, they placed him in the open plains, an environment where healthy elephants thrive. To their surprise, the elephant did not run and enjoy his freedom. He simply stayed in one place and rocked back and forth, his body still searching for the walls he'd been knocking up against all his life. He still believed that he was in his small enclosure. The elephant could not see the open field and freedom, although the enclosure no longer existed. Prison had invaded his mind to the point that he was now a prisoner of his own making. He stood in the open field of freedom but was still bound by mental chains.

Isn't that just like many of us? We have the call of leadership on our lives and yet have difficulty believing that we could be leaders. We stand as free agents here on earth. The larger we become, the more trapped we feel. An explosion is inevitable. We will either explode or implode. We have the freedom to make choices that influence our lives and the lives of those around us. We can come and go as we please. We can change jobs, clothes, and friends whenever we like, but are we really free?

Like that elephant, many of us stand in chosen enclosures of bondage and when we hear whispers of freedom, we rock to the left. When we hear whispers of peace, we rock to the right. We believe that we are still held captive in the jaws of bondage and stand paralyzed by past failures, rejections, and the harsh words and judgments of those closest to us.

We stand rocking back and forth in the open field of freedom, held fast by the chains of bondage. We allow invisible chains forged by unkind words to hold us back from our destiny. Forged by unkind tongues, these chains keep us from leading. We stand like the elephant, immobilized with fear, not realizing that we stand in a prison that no longer exists.

As an activist leader, you now have a choice. Freedom awaits your presence. By renewing your mind and focusing on your dreams and filling your life with positive people, thoughts, and words, you can silence bondage and break his power.

But it is also critical to accept what God says. Many people do not like talking about the spiritual side of humanity but we discuss it because our freedom comes from God Himself. Freedom, like the Spirit, is intangible, yet it influences how you see yourself and ultimately who you become.

Activist leader, there is greatness in you. God created you to be free. Freedom is calling you out of your invisible prison. Invisible prisons are real prisons in the spiritual realm. They are just as real as stone walls and steel bars are in a natural prison. The way you respond to the spiritual side of life can make an invisible prison as real as being behind locked doors. And like the elephant, you can stand in the open field of destiny and not reap its benefits.

As freedom calls your name, choose to answer. You cannot live a productive life without it. As you move towards the sound of freedom's voice, allow the chains to fall at your feet. The wind of freedom's power can then sweep them away and bury them in the sands of forgetfulness.

Hearing freedom's voice and then following it takes courage. It also takes faith. It takes faith to scale the wall of fear and ride the waves of change. Once the waves come, wisdom beckons you to make wise choices and wade in the deep waters.

How do you escape these invisible prisons and transition to freedom? How do you make wise choices and step into your role as a leader? The first step is accepting that beautiful, powerful person called *you*. There is no one else who can do what you do the way that you do it, and that's a fact! You must first know who you are and embrace the unshakable power of your identity. Until you can walk unashamed and not apologize for your existence or identity, you will remain unchanged.

Today, spend time alone with the One who created you and with that person called you. You can then shake off the big, floppy ears, the long trunk, the thick, gray skin, and kick down the invisible walls. This time, as you rock to your left, shatter a wall. As you rock to the right, take out some steel bars. As you stomp your feet, tear down a prison wall. As an activist leader you are called to lead others. So come out of your invisible prison and *lead*!

4

The Strategic Leader

No plan, no mission!

If you scored more B's on the Leadership Style Inventory you operate in the strategic leadership style. People often describe you as conservative and orderly when you work. You are the woman who wants everything done yesterday. You are organized, efficient, accurate, self-disciplined, and a woman who demands perfection. Order and structure are the central themes for your life and you do not apologize for what you need or want.

As a strategic leader you are a born planner. You are thorough and you usually operate with high standards. Others may try and shake you from you position, but they often have difficulty unless there are some spiritual imbalances influencing your life. When operating at your best and most efficient, you are a wonder to watch.

As a strategic leader, your first thoughts always involve planning. In your mind, there is nothing more bound for failure than a woman without a plan. Your strengths are developing standard operating procedures, policy manuals, and rules of order in any organization. The first thing you look for as a new employee is the benefits manual. You want to know what benefits belongs to you and how to access those benefits should you need them.

You also want to understand the parameters surrounding your job responsibilities. It is important that you to know where they begin and end. You want to avoid all conflict and know that standing on another person's turf can ignite conflict faster than any forest fire. You do not want to get caught in one those fires and you do all within your power to avoid them.

Honor, respect, and fairness are your leadership codes. You try to treat everyone as fairly as you can, but you also realize that it is not always possible. Because of your unique ability to discern trouble before it starts, you ask for help from other team members. You make sure to stay connected with team members who are creative in their thinking and solicit suggestions when faced with challenges in this area. Your domain is the policy manual. Their domain is people management.

Strategic Leadership Strengths

You are at your best during a crisis. As a Strategic leader, you have the ability to compartmentalize your emotions and move forward toward solutions. You have no fear when it comes to facing the challenges associated with a crisis. Your conduct usually dissipates fears because you can give concise directions without pause. You and fear cannot coexist. If fear decides to visit you and any mission you are leading, then you are the first to face him and send him running to look for an easier target.

Others describe you as commanding, authoritative, and definitely in charge. At first glance these traits may appear to be masculine, but you are far from that. You can wear a skirt, spray on your favorite perfume, and give orders with the best of men. You have no problem displaying the strength of your femininity while giving hard orders to complete a mission. And as far as handling a difficult mission goes, you are just the woman to handle it.

In your eyes, gender has nothing to do with competency. Your focus is the mission at hand and you will not allow others to brand it with their limited perceptions regarding gender. To you, leadership is leadership. Leading others, as long as you have a plan, is the ultimate goal. What others say has little impact on you and your decisions, especially if they are unwilling to take a leadership position. You have little patience and no respect for those who stand around and complain, appearing to be fearful of leadership's mantle.

You delight in giving clear directions and have no problem with authority. You believe that the authority to execute comes with a leadership position. You may appear to be cold or unfeeling to others, but this far from the truth. You do have feelings but once given a mission, the mission becomes your target. You then realize that you do not have time to waste on how you or others feel about it. You just execute. You do not need agreement from others—just compliance and then action. This approach serves you well in times of crisis when you need unquestioned rapid action and with problem employees who do not respond to other methods.

You thrive in areas that depend upon attention to detail and expect others who work with you to have the same appreciation, if not the same skills. But remember that others may not appreciate your focus and attention on minutiae. They may consider it nitpicky or a hindrance to forward movement. What many of your team members do not know is that the very details they detest may be the very things that save them during a crisis in the mission.

When you design a plan, you expect others to follow it to the letter without deviation. One of your strengths is being able to see over the next mountain where danger and traps set by the enemy can quickly arise. You plan for the unexpected and expect your team members to have the correct tools for any unexpected events.

Deborah

She was the warrior-judge!

> Deborah, the wife of Lappidoth, was a prophet who
> was judging Israel at that time. She would sit under the
> Palm of Deborah, between Ramah and Bethel in the hill
> country of Ephraim, and the Israelites would go to her
> for judgment (Judges 4:4-5)

Picture yourself sitting under a flourishing palm tree that bears
your name. This tree is where you sit every day doing your job...
every day except the Sabbath, of course! Your job? You are a judge
of Israel. You watch daily as a multitude comes before you for counsel. You settle disputes, sanction agreements, bless babies, and oversee the everyday activities of your people. You have your hands full...
full of God's people, that is! Boredom is something you seldom see
since activity makes your life his playground. You love what you do
and understand the great responsibility that comes with your territory. The pressure is great but you are able to withstand it because
you have God's grace enabling you to do what you do.

As if you needed more pressure, on this beautiful morning you
had to call for the commander of Israel's army. You know that he has
disobeyed God and has not deployed his army against an imposing
enemy. Although you have people waiting, this situation can go on
no longer. You summon him without delay.

"Barack, didn't the Lord God of Israel tell you to go and deploy
troops at Mount Tabor? You were to take ten thousand men and go
to the Kishon river and face Sisera, the commander of Jabin's army
and his chariots. The Lord said that He would deliver him into your
hands! Is this fear I see?"

The commander shakes with dread as he wonders how he and his
army can fight this approaching iron-clad war machine. With terror

holding him captive, the commander then speaks the unspeakable. He will not go out to face this enemy unless you go with him to war.

Iron chariots! An enemy's army! You've got things to do and people to see and this man is worried about chariots?

Standing before you are hundreds of people who need answers to family emergencies and counsel. God has already told this man that He will give him victory and yet he hesitates. You can hardly believe that fear rules the military and that this commander will not face the enemy without you.

You tell him that if you have to go then the coming victory will not belong to him, but instead be given to a woman. He seems undisturbed by this revelation so you accompany him to the battlefield. You have no fear of swords or chariots. You have no fear of the enemy who hides behind his iron shield.

You watch as victory embraces your army and as a woman's hand defeats this angry tyrant. You realize that things happening are beyond your control and that again, you have been given a great gift. You have seen the miraculous! You also remember that you have not prepared dinner, but you understand that victory is sometimes made of uncooked meals.

On that day, your strategic sister Deborah commanded Barack to take Israel's army onto the field and the Lord gave Israel the battle. Sisera fled on foot and ran to the tent of Jael, the wife of Heber the Kenite. He asked her for something to drink and a place to hide. She gave him milk and hid him under a blanket in her tent. He asked her to then guard him, which she did.

Once he was safely under the blanket, Jael took a hammer and drove a tent peg through his temple. She then informed Israel's army of her conquest. Sisera, just as Deborah had predicted, died by the hand of a woman. With Israel's enemy defeated, Jabin's kingdom was also later destroyed.

Deborah was a woman of greatness. She spoke God's word and commanded Barack to lead the army against a foe that was said to be unbeatable. She was without fear and was the only woman to serve as a judge in Israel. She not only spoke words of wisdom and gave counsel; she also led an army to war since its commander was afraid to lead. Like you, her strategic sister, she followed God's plan and embraced victory!

Strategic Leadership Style Challenges

Since you are conservative and orderly, you may appear to be impatient to others. You are not usually impatient. You just like things done correctly. After it's done correctly, you then want everything done...yesterday. This may irritate less structure-driven people. They may want to stretch the rules or make changes that violate policies and procedures, but you will have no part of this. You realize that this attitude may cause conflict, but you are willing to pay the price of being unpopular. Your biggest concern is getting it right, no matter what the cost.

Others soon learn that this is what you bring to the table. And your attitude is that it's okay for you to be you. Your leadership style actually protects the organization and individual.

Structure, order, and systems are your life themes. As a strategic leader, you like working in structured environments with standard operation procedures and rules of conduct. Because of these traits, you thrive when given authority or management of people, places or things. The more authority you have, the more you thrive.

Because you are comfortable with authority, people often misjudge you and your actions because they believe that you are domineering. Nothing could be further from the truth. It's just that you operate well within well-defined systems. Most systems have strict boundaries and you understand and like boundaries more than any other leadership style.

Operating as a Strategic leader, remember that you are unique in that others rely on you for your knowledge of operating procedures. They rely on you to help them recognize the true traits of prospective job applicants when selecting others for promotion or project managers.

Remember that your gifts are needed in the workplace. There will always be people who will not like to follow rules, but know that your sense of order and discipline are necessary components of a successful workplace.

What do you accept? What do you believe? Do you accept that you are a gift to someone? Do you believe that you were created for a magnificent purpose? Do you accept that you are an answer to someone's prayer? Do you accept that there is no one like you who can do what you do the way that you do it? Believe it because it's true. So accept the wonder of who you are and what you bring to life's table! Believe it. Embrace it. Accept it.

Madam C.J. Walker

I am a woman who came from the cotton fields of the South. From there I was promoted to the washtub. From there I was promoted to the cook kitchen. And from there I promoted myself into the business of manufacturing hair goods and preparations....I have built my own factory on my own ground. —Madam Walker, National Negro Business League Convention, July 1912

"I'll have more orders for you next week. There are a few more ladies I didn't get the chance to talk to today and I know they need to do their hair," Clarissa said with a giggle.

"Clarissa, you are such a gift. Girl, you know just how to help these women. You know that we all love looking good," said Sarah.

"Well, when I come back next week, I'm going to need to sample some of your other products too. Since this hair treatment worked so well, I want to see everything."

Clarissa turned and left. *That Clarissa is so good with bringing me customers,* Sarah thought to herself. *Good customers. I wish there was some way I could repay her other than with a quick thank-you. She works so hard and she deserves so much more. What can I do? She faithfully brings me at least ten new customers every month. That's at least sixty new paying customers over the last six months. Wait a minute. I believe I've got it!*

She opened her notebook and began writing. The intensity of the idea burning within her nearly scorched the pages. With each stroke of her pen, she could see the design of her plan coming to life. This was not going to be easy, but she had learned a long time ago that anything worth having was never easy. Knowing this only made her more determined to make her idea a reality. Sitting in her parlor on that warm day, Sarah Breedlove, better known as Madam C.J. Walker, could never have imagined that she was crafting history.

She stroked her long, curly hair and remembered that it had not always been so beautiful. There were days she ran her fingers through here tresses and discovered tender places on her scalp. As a young woman, she experimented with lotions, creams, and tonics until she found the right combination. It took weeks for her see a difference but finally she had the bald spots running for cover underneath the new hair growth. Once she saw how it worked and knew that she had the right formula, she shared it with other women.

By the time she finished, she had developed several products, including Wonderful Hair Grower, Glossine pressing oil for straightening hair, and Vegetable Shampoo. She sold her products door-to-door and instructed her customers on how to use them. Her customers loved the service and became a strong force in spreading the word.

After several days of intense writing, editing, and calculations, this daughter of former slaves completed the plan. As she checked over every detail to ensure that the numbers were correct, she could barely contain herself. Just thinking of the numerous women's lives she could touch made her want to dance around the room and shout. She knew that what she developed was completely ingenious and that the end result would be fair not only to her, but to Clarissa as well. Nervousness and fear tried to strangle this tender plant of an idea but she fought both with pen and ink. Hesitation and doubt tried to rob her mind but she waged war with prayer and wise words older women had taught her. All she had to do now was get Clarissa to accept it.

Clarissa is such a jewel and I am so excited about this plan. I just hope she is too. She should make some money too! Why not? She's doing the work. When she gets here next week, I pray that she accepts my offer.

"Well, come in Clarissa. It's so wonderful to see you. With that big smile on your face, you must have some good news. How many orders do you have this week?"

"It's good to see you too, Madam C.J. I have something to tell you," Clarissa said as she tried to catch her breath. She had run down the block and one could see that the wind had been dancing in her hair the entire way there.

"Well, what is girl? What happened?" Madam C.J. stopped in her tracks and turned to face Clarissa.

"I cannot believe what has happened. This week has been incredible! I have forty-five orders! Can you believe it? Women just love your products and I don't mind coming here for the pick-up and delivering them. It just makes them better mothers, wives, sisters, and friends when they feel good about themselves. And your products help with that in such a big way," responded Clarissa.

"Then what I have to talk with you about couldn't have come at a better time." Of course, Clarissa accepted her offer and began selling the hair products to her customers and making money. The entrepreneurial woman who developed this system did not realize that by creating this method, she was also creating a business model that would become one of the top income generating methods of modern day business.

Madam C.J. Walker empowered other women by allowing them to purchase her products at wholesale prices and sell them at retail to their customers. She trained and offered opportunities to numerous women who, in turn, offered it to other women. All the while, Madam Walker made money on every purchase and she helped women become financially empowered while staying home with their children.

She trained each woman on how to demonstrate and then sell the products. She trained each woman on how to spot women who had a passion for the products and then how to offer them the opportunity to be business partners and share in the profits. She personally packed each box for her business partners and coached them weekly on how to run their businesses. She designed the packaging with the thousands of women who became her customers in mind. What joy it gave her to see other women financially empowered and still raise their families.

Madam C.J. Walker designed a business system that is still being taught in halls of higher learning in the top business schools in the world. Corporations today use her model to generate billions of dollars of revenue. And to top it off, the daughter of former slaves became the first self-made female millionaire in the United States.

Long before women like Mary Kay Ash and Estee Lauder entered the world of beauty, Madam C.J. Walker paved the road for them to walk on in the world of feminine success. This woman made history and money. Not a bad combination for a strategic leader!

Strategic Leadership Tips

Be yourself!

Remember, there is no one like you. There is no need for you to accept any pressure to change who you are and how you operate. What most people don't understand is that consistency and order are necessary facets of success. You have that part down to a science. So don't be ashamed of offering your gift at mission's table. It is needed more than you know.

Remember that there is no one who can do what you do the way that you do it. There will always be misunderstandings with others. Use your gift to diffuse it. There will always be conflict. Just stay in your lane. You cannot change others. You control only how you respond. Your job is to keep your own life in order. If someone wants your counsel or has need of your gifts of order and consistency they will ask. Just continue to be the original you.

Remember that others do not always see things in the same light as you.

Even if you explain every detail of a situation to some people, they may not understand the inner workings of the situation. Just do what you can and then leave the rest for them to figure out. Although you are a problem solver by nature, you cannot solve everything for everyone. If you take on too much of an emotional load, then you could lose your balance. This could lead to your not being as influential when using your gifts. You can only deliver messages and hope others will listen.

If others decide not to receive them, you cannot force the issue. Remember that you have a keen sense of discernment so others may see what you see while still not understanding your language.

You know the rules.

Others don't always know what you know because they may not possess the same gifts. Since your focus is order, you may already know the rules and regulations that govern your workplace. You may even be the author of those rules and regulations. This gives you an inner view that others may not ever see. You understand the behind-the-scenes reasons for the policies. You understand the reasons the organization developed their procedures and you also understand how team members can protect themselves if they choose to follow the established policies and procedures.

Just remember that not everyone takes the time to read and research procedures. Just make gentle suggestions to help others so that they will not come to resent you and your knowledge.

The Strategic Leader and the Five Leadership Facets

Leadership Facet 1: Activation/Ignition

For you mission is like driving a luxury vehicle. While you believe in traveling in style, everyone who rides must devote time and attention to the vehicle. Once the vehicle is road-ready, the mission can begin. For you activation is planning because you can then determine the best way to arrive at your desired destination.

Since you are the consummate planner and every detail must be mapped out in order to begin, you check out all routes to your destination. You advise team members to do the same. Once everyone sits at the table, you scan each route or idea to make the best decision for the team. Once you receive information and feedback from your team, you write the plan. Then, and only then, can the strategic leader have ignition.

Leadership Facet 2: Shifting into Gear/Direction

GPS is critical for you. It gives directions and creates a clear path to your destination. All strategic shifting involves planning. You will not start a mission without clear directions and the necessary resources. Before you shift the mission into gear you have to know that there is a true purpose behind it.

You must also know what resources you will need and where you can acquire them. You do not have the time or energy to search for what you need while engaged in the mission. When a driver shifts a car into gear, she is the singular force deciding where the car will go. After you accept a mission, you and your team will decide on the best course of action. The only way for you to make clear, logical decisions is to have a solid plan with solid team members to assist in the execution of that plan.

Leadership Facet 3: Inspiration (Motivation)/Acceleration

Inspiration is usually not one of your strengths. You rely on others with the gift of exhortation to assist you in this area. It's not that you don't desire to inspire your team; it's that you focus on mission-readiness and execution. If you inspire someone, it is usually by your actions. You want others to know that you do appreciate them but a job well done should speak for itself.

Partnering with team members who have a gift for inspiring and encouraging others, you make a vital connection. You allow the gifted team members to do what they do. And you allow that gift to flow to assist the team. You continue to focus on what you need to do and where you need to go.

Leadership Facet 4: Training and Development/Fueling

You always have a training plan. For you, training is like breathing. There is no way you can execute a plan without first training your team. It is critical that every member understand just how important she is to the mission. This can only be accomplished by training.

Although you may have already developed a plan, you are still open to input from your team. You obtain this feedback during the training process. You can see what works and what does not work when put into action during training. When the actual mission occurs, you will have already worked out the kinks in the process because you put together thorough training sessions for your team.

As a strategic leader, you understand that training must work hand-in-hand with your plan in order for success to be a part of your mission song!

Leadership Facet 5: Rewards and Recognition/Maintenance

As a strategic leader, you have no problem recognizing team members for a job well done. You are tough but fair. If you see great effort presented by a team member, you also expect great fruit. Even if they do not meet their personal goals, you will still recognize and reward them for trying. You ensure that they receive more training if needed to assist them in their next attempt should they fall short of where they wanted to go.

You help them to see what actions need to be corrected or what skills need to be sharpened. You roll up your sleeves and offer assistance. You may not have the words they need to hear, but you do have the necessary actions, equipment, and training. You leave the exhortation and encouragement to others who have the gift. This way, you allow others with different gifts to also shine in the rewards and recognition department.

Anne Graham Lotz

"When we face an impossible situation, all self-reliance and self-confidence must melt away; we must be totally dependent on Him (Jesus) for the resources." With this statement, Anne Graham Lotz shows women today that before they can lead, they must first understand that Jesus must be the center in all they say and do. It's not difficult to see why she speaks the way she does. One can see God's fingerprints on every facet of her life.

Imagine growing up in the magnificent mountains of North Carolina surrounded by lush green hills and snow-capped peaks. As if that weren't enough, her parents are world-famous evangelist Billy Graham and Ruth Graham. Anne was exposed to leadership firsthand. Her father served as a spiritual advisor to leaders, including many presidents of the United States.

Her mother, according to her father, was the best Bible teacher he knew and she was the only person he turned to for spiritual counsel. Godly examples of leadership filled Anne's life.

One can easily see that her faith in Jesus is the center of her life. She accepted the Lord at age eight after watching the Cecil B. DeMille movie *Kings of Kings*. Little did she know that this decision would color her life and lives of others with God's marvelous grace through the work she would do.

Anne married just out of high school and moved to Raleigh, North Carolina, with her new husband, Dr. Danny Lotz. They have been married for over 46 years.

While still a young wife and mother, Anne began teaching for Bible Study Fellowship in Raleigh. Before she taught, she waited for over a year for someone else to step up and teach in her city. When no one came forward, she began teaching. Her class quickly filled up and she had an attendance of over five hundred with a waiting list. She did this for twelve years. While teaching, she started receiving many speaking invitations. As a result of those requests and her leaving her position with Bible Study Fellowship, she created AnGeL Ministries.

Although there was some resistance to her ministry from conservative Christians, she still drew in large crowds from her speaking. The *New York Times* even once called her one of the five most influential evangelists of her generation in the United States.

Anne's ministry changed when her family called. In the span of two years a hurricane destroyed her husband's dental office and her mother's health began failing. She required several hospitalizations. All three of Anne's children married within eight months and one of her sons was diagnosed with cancer. Just as she had in times past, she focused on her family and turned to God's Word for comfort and direction. This time, her study resulted in her writing the best-selling book *Just Give Me Jesus*.

Your sister strategic leader Anne Graham Lotz is a beautiful example of feminine leadership. Like you, she listens when God speaks and understands that there will be times when you may not feel comfortable when and where He calls you. But He always calls you to places of abundance!

5

The Tactical Leader

No flexibility, no mission.

If you scored more C's on the Leadership Style Inventory you operate in the Tactical Leadership style. People often describe you as self-confident, commanding, organized, forceful, motivated, and diligent. Others may also call you energized, a risk taker, and unpredictable. You are gifted in handling conflict and have the ability to see both sides of a situation and help others do the same. You can see the gifts of others and help them find their correct place when working on a mission.

As a Tactical leader, you are a born people manager. Your leadership style has a highly positive impact on organizational climate. You motivate, encourage, nurture, and push your team to victory. One of your strengths is sharing the credit for a job well done with your team members. The reason you are able to do this without hesitation is because in most situations, you started in a lower position and had to work your way to the top.

You are the leader who started as a secretary and ended up managing the entire department. You learned the organization from the ground up and have no problem conversing with team members at all levels. This is one of the reasons you can get into doors that are closed to others. You nurture the gatekeepers like no other leader. You understand the flow of power and have no problem identifying and accessing it to get what you need when you need it.

You have the unique ability to sell or market what you are doing to such a degree that others believe what you say. You are just that convincing. You are also skilled at gaining entry into doors closed to others to get the job done.

As a tactical leader, you love a challenge. When given a challenge, you can and will meet it, assuming you are allowed flexibility in completing the mission. For you, flexibility is synonymous with authority. If you are not given the authority to execute, you cannot move forward with your mission. It has to bear your signature in order for you to see success. Once given the necessary orders to develop a plan that suits your style, you execute. When someone gives you a mission with a challenge you will see it through to the end, but only if you are allowed flexibility as you do so.

Tactical Leadership Strengths

You have presence. Whenever you enter a room, you change the atmosphere without uttering a word. You are the type of person who people either love or hate. The people who hate you cannot, when confronted, tell you why they dislike you. They just know that your very presence irritates them. For some, it may be that your self-confidence comes across as arrogance.

There is nothing farther from the truth. You are the person who sees the glass as half full instead of half empty. Your positive outlook irritates those who see the glass as half empty. It doesn't bother you because you thrive where differences of opinion exist. You realize that everyone brings something of interest to the table and that's where you find solutions. The differences help you to better see hidden facts or less apparent ways of doing things. In others words, the differences help you to learn new and exciting information.

Other people with different views do not bother you, nor do those who dislike you for no apparent reason. You can usually spot these people and try to stay out of their way when you can. Develop your own strategy for dealing with them.

You have a strong need to connect with your team members. You also have an intense desire to use organizational goals as the core of your planning and execution and have no problem letting others know where you stand.

You also enjoy holding long conversations with others that extend outside the office. These are not just mere conversations. They are also assessments. You use the knowledge gained to help others find their strengths and weaknesses. You are an expert at helping them identify and then connect these gifts to their actions, assisting them with career success and development.

You are excellent at delegating and enjoy watching others learn a new skill. You delight in giving a challenging assignment to your team and then observing how they solve challenges. You applaud them for every challenge met and then roll up your sleeves and show them how to meet the others.

You have the unique ability to see the gifts of others and not be intimidated by those gifts. You delight in seeing others soar! Because of this quality, you have very few incidents of disloyalty because your team members know you are willing to practice what you preach.

You are a great leader and understand the power of working with a team but also see those individual skills and abilities are critical elements to success. You know that it takes a network of powerful people to accomplish any mission. You help those who can only see the mission feel the heart of others, and you can help those who wear their hearts on their sleeves to see the importance of focusing on the mission.

Esther

You discover a plot to kill everyone dear to you and the only thing that can stop death's savage approach is for you to break the law and risk death. The order has been signed. A date has been set. Death's tidal wave will overtake the region.

You can hardly believe it. But instead of becoming distraught, you decide to stop eating for three days. You inform your maidservants that they must support you by joining you on your extended fast. Everyone around you must participate in your quest. After the days of fasting are over, you bathe, comb your hair, put on your best perfume, and adorn yourself in your most lavish dress.

You have decided to step into fear's arena unafraid. Fear cannot have his way with you on this day because you are a woman on a mission. You are fighting for a cause bigger than yourself. You are fighting for the survival of a people.

The power of the moment embraces you and an Unseen Force places His hand in the small of your back and pushes you forward. Without the slightest hesitation, you then walk boldly into an open forum into the presence of the one who signed the unjust death order. You stand before him waiting and hoping for a miracle, knowing that if he chooses not to give mercy, the law says that you must die. You must die because he did not send for you. The law says that the only way to come into his presence is for him to summon you.

As you stand before him, you realize that the only thing standing between you and death is an act of power on his part. You pray that he sees your heart. You know how things work, but you know that with God's help the king will see your true intent. You also hope that he will catch the scent of your perfume and remember the nights spent together. You pray that he sees you not as a woman who has violated the law but as a queen with a need so great that only her king can meet it.

Holding your breath and drinking in the moment, you bow your head and glance at his face, and there you see the unexpected. You see the glimmer in his eyes and you watch delight dance in his heart as he looks upon you. You then behold a transformation. He relaxes his shoulders and his posture changes. He is not the ruler of the empire, but just a man in love.

You then experience the miraculous. He extends his golden scepter and asks you to come closer so that he can hear your request. Just as death whispers your name, your king calls you back into the court of life. His voice overcomes death and you walk toward him in your royal robe.

You can barely speak because in that moment, his words saved you from certain doom. He lifts his voice and offers you up to half his kingdom if you would but tell him what is in your heart. In that moment, you also know that every movement and every word from this moment forward must be executed with tactical precision in order for you to achieve your goal.

On that day, your tactical sister Queen Esther risked her life by coming before the king without being summoned. Although she knew that by law she was forbidden to do so, she had little choice. She was a Jew and the edict stated that all the Jews were to die. As queen, she had little choice but to act and realized that her position gave her access to power; access to the king.

Her cousin Mordecai sent a message to her that a death sentence was signed for the Jewish people, and that if she remained silent God would bring deliverance another way. But, he added, he believed that God had brought Esther to the royal throne for such a time as this. Queen Esther was resolved, and she decided to move forward.

Your tactical leader sister devised and executed a multifaceted plan and spoke words that still reverberate through the halls of history. "If I perish, I perish," she said as she prepared to go before her king.

In the end she saved her people. In tactical leadership style, she boldly faced death by risking her life and won not only the heart of a king but the love of a nation.

Challenges of the Tactical Leader

While others usually describe you as self-confident, motivated, and organized in your method of operation, they can also use the words *unpredictable*. At first glance, others may want to follow you to the ends of the earth but they can back out of a project once they learn that you just volunteered to spend the next year in Antarctica!

For you, there is no in between. Since they have no real reason for their dislike, you must keep focused on what you've been called to do. If you stop and try to investigate or try to change the person's mind, you are inviting trouble. You are also hindering the mission by focusing on personalities rather than getting the job done.

You use the policies and procedures manual and research how and if you can do certain things. You will push the organizational parameters if they interfere with your personal agenda and with the way you believe a mission should flow.

This can be problematic, especially if the policy you challenge has long been in place and those in power can see no reason for making the change. Not a problem for you because you are just the woman to show them the error in their thinking.

While your suggestion could make things easier or make the work flow more smoothly, study the situation before rushing in with your new idea. Take time to research the reasons the organization developed the policy and how changing it would impact every aspect of the organizational structure. Ensure that it will not cause job loss or negatively impact the financial bottom line.

Although you delight in helping others use their gifts and talents, you also have a tendency to push them before they are ready to move. This action could be mislabeled as micromanaging when your intent was to encourage.

You will take on what appears to be an impossible project and succeed where others fail. Although this is a strength, it can also be classified as a challenge. You and your team can pay a heavy price for your commitment. Remember that family, friends, and relationships suffer when you focus too intently on a mission and make it your life instead of your work. Many tactical leaders have lost or damaged significant relationships for the sake of a mission.

Continue to use your gift of helping diverse groups work well together in spite of their differences. It is one of your most powerful weapons against division. Also remember to give quality time to your relationships. These things keep you strong and sharp. These things keep you at your tactical best. As a Tactical leader, you can shape and change your world with your style and grace like no other!

If you are ready for change, then you have to do something different. It's time to jump! Jump with both feet! Jump into something you've always wanted but were afraid to try. Jump into a new relationship you never really explored. It won't wait forever and tomorrow is not promised to you. So jump! While you still can and while you still have the desire, leap into life! That's what leaders do!

Queen Nzinga of Angola

Imagine watching as giant, ominous, floating birds fill the

horizon near the shores of your homeland. These monsters then stop short of the beach and strange men with white skin come ashore. They stroll on the beach as if your land belonged to them.

They set up their tents and cut down your trees and begin to build compounds. They take what they want without asking; not even acknowledging your people's presence. It's as if they have no fear. They appear to be workers of evil because they ignore the natural beauty that surrounds them and rape the land of resources.

You speak to your brother the king and ask him to speak to these invaders. He refuses, but you do not give up. At your urging, your brother approaches the strangers. They sign a treaty when they realize they cannot penetrate the defenses leading to the interior of your country. These men call themselves Dutchmen.

But you soon learn that a new group has landed. They are different from the other men. These men call themselves the Portuguese. Like the Dutchmen, they rape the land but they are much crueler in their doings. These Portuguese then begin to do the unthinkable. They seize your people and use them as slaves to help build their houses and fortresses. After they finish the building, they place the people into the belly of their strange birds and sail away with them. Their families never see them again for these evil men have taken them as human cargo. You soon realize that these Portuguese find no value in your homeland except what they can take.

You can bear it no longer. Your brother the king does nothing but speak in fear. He talks with these Portuguese and signs a treaty with them, giving them access to other tribes and people. You watch as your brother continues to make concessions to these Portuguese. All the while, your anger boils within you like a volcano.

All the surrounding kingdoms have the same fears. Can they not see that if they banded together they could defeat this foe? You petition the chiefs of neighboring villages to unite with your region to run these strange, impolite intruders out of your lands.

Fear fills their hearts and they can see the weapons of these invaders. The chiefs believe there is no way to defeat them and drive them back into the sea from whence they came. You devise a plan which could take some time, but that does not matter. You have to make a decision that will change the face of your nation. You decide to go to war against these evil men but need more time and a tactical plan.

You convince your brother to allow you to respond to an audience with the Portuguese governor. Dressed in your royal regalia, you and your royal company arrive at his office only to find that he will not offer you a seat. Seated behind his desk, he begins to speak to you as if you were one of his servants. You interrupt his speech by clapping your hands. At the sound of your clap, your maidservant bows before you. And since no seat was offered, you use her as a human seat.

The Dutch historian records that there would be no easy victory for the Portuguese. A woman who holds the respect and honor even of her foes is a force to be reckoned with. Both the Dutch and the Portuguese were in for the fight of their lives facing the mighty Queen Nzinga of Angola, your tactical leader sister. Both nations invaded Angola. The Dutch were unable to penetrate the interior of the country. Nzinga, in the midst of dealing with the invaders, learned of the new faith these invaders possessed. She decided to convert to Christianity. To her surprise, her conversion and new faith meant nothing to the invaders. They continued on their blood-thirsty quest to enslave the people of her region.

The brutality of the Portuguese instilled fear into the hearts of the regional tribes. Because of Portuguese pressure and the demand for concessions with the slave trade, her brother, the king of the Mbundu people, committed suicide. Nzinga then became queen. Queen Nzinga refused to allow the Portuguese to rule or control her and her nation. She negotiated a treaty with neighboring kingdoms to join her in war. She then led a united army against the Portuguese. This started a war that lasted for over thirty years.

She then entered into a treaty with the Dutch, exploiting European rivalries. Together they fought and defeated the Portuguese. When the Portuguese defeated the Dutch the following year, the Dutch left the region. Queen Nzinga continued to lead her army against the Portuguese using guerilla warfare tactics. The Portuguese could barely believe that a woman could lead with such power. This so angered them that they placed a bounty on her head. Nzinga led her warriors into battle until well into her sixties. She told everyone to call her king instead of queen because she was a ruler.

When the Portuguese began to overrun the villages, Nzinga and her warriors hid in the hills and began a campaign of guerilla warfare. They soon realized that spears were no match for the guns and artillery of the Portuguese. The invaders soon overtook the people and began a savage slave trade.

The Portuguese made many attempts to capture or kill this Christian queen but were never able to do so. She died peacefully in her sleep at the age of eighty. Your Tactical leader sister Queen Nzinga led her troops in the war against slavery until she was in her sixties and influenced her future countrymen to fight until they won their independence in 1975. The wave of her influence lasted until centuries later when her countrymen won their independence by using the same guerilla warfare tactics she used against the earlier Portuguese army. Now, that's tactical leadership at its best!

Tactical Leadership Tips

Do not allow others to pull you into disagreements.

Unnecessary fights waste your time and energy. Because of your love of fairness, you will try and see what you could have done to prevent the chaos. Although it may not be your fault, you will end up "looping" and the end result with be missed opportunities. You can keep yourself so busy putting out fires that you may forget to make necessary phone calls and follow-up appointments. The bottom line is not to allow others to steal your time and energy.

You have such fire that it may appear to be endless. Complaining, whining, and unnecessary warfare consumes your fire. You are a powerful woman and the quickest way to deplete your power is to be pulled into needless battles. Choose your battles wisely. Take the time to look over each incident to see if it's really worth your time and effort. Review how it will best serve you or your organization. You can feel the flow if things begin to sap your energy supply. Save your power. Polish your armor for encounters that really matter.

Don't change your style for anyone.

Your presence is a gift. Don't allow others to tell you to tone yourself down unless you can see that you really need to do it. You have panache and there is nothing wrong with it. It is gift from God, so use it in His service.

If your presence is causing you to lose business or friends, then check yourself. It may be attributed to envy but it could be something more. Just watch how you use your gift. There are many who will be threatened by it. But for the most part, it shouldn't be a hindrance to your business, especially since most of your clients do business with you because of your style.

There are times when we have to watch how others react to us but it doesn't mean that we need to change who we are. Study the business culture and do what you do best…improvise! You are a genius in using your gifts to complement others.

Be slow to act and slower still to judge.

There are times when you may misjudge the actions of others. If you hear someone criticize the company, you may believe that the person is not a loyal employee. It may be that the person was just having a bad day and their problem was not actually with the job.

When you see someone mistreat another person, you may record this error in judgment as a permanent character trait of the person involved. Watch and learn. People are not perfect and tend to bring their personal issues to work. Take a deep breath and watch and wait before you say or do anything.

The Tactical Leader and the Five Leadership Facets

Leadership Facet 1: Activation/Ignition

You are a leader who understands ignition like no other. Your middle name is ignition because you ignite those around you with mission's fire. You have no problem explaining why, where, or what you and your team needs to do. You use creative words and phrases to create your unique mission environment and your team enjoys the journey with you in charge.

During times when you don't feel the ignition, you have already appointed others with the gift to take the lead. Ignition is never a challenge with your group. Everyone on your team will have their turn at inspiring and motivating the team to mission success. And you are the right leader for getting the job started!

Leadership Facet 2: Shifting into Gear/Direction

As a Tactical leader, you understand that proper direction is one of the keys to mission success. Planning is critical, but if you run into speed bumps along the path you can still handle the job. You enjoy building in flexibility to any plan to ensure that the end result will be best for your team and the organization.

If a team member suggests a different direction and it does not interfere with the end result, you are open. You believe that with every new idea there is a new lesson to be learned. With every lesson there is a new realm of discovery.

Leadership Facet 3: Inspiration (Motivation)/Acceleration

You love doing what you do and, like any leader, your work is your map. Like a powerful general, you study the history of a situation and then you adapt your course of actions according to the unique personalities and needs of your team and your organization.

You have no problem with moving forward although many times you may not have all the necessary information. That could be problematic for some leadership styles but for you, operating in your tactical style, it is no problem. You move forward and adapt while picking up what you need as you go.

You will stop and assess without excuse because there are times when moving could be detrimental. As a tactical leader, you want nothing more than success. You've learned to move at a pace where you can control the direction and resources. Tactical wisdom is the only way to go for you.

Leadership Facet 4: Training and Development /Fueling

You are the consummate trainer. You want your team members to know how to do their jobs with excellence. You believe cross training is a necessary part of mission readiness. If someone has a job and they are unable to perform, there is no reason that their job should go undone. Another team member should be ready to step in without hesitation. The only way this happens is with training. Every person on your team will know the job of all their team members so that there are no gaps in the mission being complete. If this doesn't happen then you believe the team is not in a state of readiness.

Every team member has a training manual and you direct them to read it thoroughly. You give impromptu testing to ensure that their skills stay sharp. This initially may not endear you to your team but after seeing the results while working on a project, they come to appreciate your methods.

Leadership Facet 5: Rewards and Recognition/Maintenance

Rewarding others for a job well done is never a problem for you. You frequently make use of the established reward systems in your organization. If an organizational award does not exist for a specific performance then you create an award. You have seen and experienced the benefits of rewarding others for a job well done. You have also experienced the pain of not being rewarded or recognized and will not inflict this upon your team members.

Being a tactical leader has its challenges, but rewarding others is never on that list. You are one of the first to volunteer to serve on the recognition committee because of your sharp eye for character. You also easily see how support staff plays a critical part in the completion of a project. You believe that recognition is for all levels of team members, from management to support staff. The title is unimportant when it comes to hard work. Effort is what really matters.

Thelma Wells

"Eyes have not seen nor have ears heard what the Father is going to do with you. You have such an amazing anointing, and girl, you ain't seen nothin' yet! Just watch and see what God does with your life," she said as she leaned over and whispered in my ear. Her white hair glistened in the morning sunlight and her smile cut through the fog that held my mind captive with doubt. She had no idea that oppression danced in my head and that pain gripped my heart. I believed what she said but there was still so much that seemed to stand in my way.

I smiled a half smile as she continued speaking words of power and blessing to me. I was accustomed to being around other women leaders and understood the culture. We had a form of sisterly love but I had never experienced anyone quite like this woman before.

Although she is petite in stature, her spirit fills a room like a joyful tidal wave. Her colorful personality illuminates the darkest of moods and she never meets a stranger. She always has a kind word for everyone she encounters, no matter what their age or background. She walks with such a combination of confidence and love that one automatically knows that she could part the Red Sea of controversy without much effort. She so freely gives of herself that it nearly consumes me whenever I am in her presence.

An expert at developing leaders, she has put together empowering gatherings for women. The work that goes into these sessions would drain a woman half her age. Her energy is contagious. Her smile is miraculous. Her love, transforming. No one can help but respond to her.

But one of the most amazing things about this woman is her faith in God and how He helped her to overcome the painful episodes of her past. All one has to do is hear her speak the powerful words of her biographical story.

"I was born Baby Girl Morris. My mother was a crippled teenager. My father was married, but not to my mother." No one would ever believe that this was the birth of a tactical leader, but Thelma Wells, or Mama T as she is fondly called, founder and CEO of A Woman of God Ministries, knows firsthand the transformative power of the true and living God.

When she was born, her grandmother made her mother leave home and find another place for her and Baby Girl Morris to live. Her mother worked as a live-in maid for a time, and after a while sent Baby Girl to live with her great-grandparents.

They loved her dearly and gave her the name of Thelma Louise Smith. They took little Thelma to church, where she heard songs of praise and hymns. She loved the music but did not realize that her young spirit would come to need them in days to come.

When she went to stay with her grandmother—the same woman who was abusive to her mother—she would lock little Thelma in a dark, insect-infested closet with no food or water. Young Thelma then used those very songs of praise to connect with God. She sang herself to sleep many days while in the closet. Her grandmother would take her out just before her grandfather came home from work and clean her up as if nothing had happened. These things were hidden from the eyes of man but not from God's eyes.

God used those songs as a spiritual healing balm and left Thelma's heart free from bitterness and anger. He rewarded her with a life filled with love, acceptance, success, and gifts to guide others out of their storms. Because of her life experiences, she is unafraid of the enemy and is the first to intercede for those who need to hear from the Father.

Thelma is an extraordinary leader, international speaker, and author. She was the first black woman in the South to establish a consulting and speaking organization. She became the first black female professor at Master's International School of Divinity in Evanston, Indiana. She also served as the first black core speaker for the Women of Faith Conferences, one of the largest women's conferences in the United States.

One can say many things about Thelma Wells and her accomplishments, but she will be the first to tell you that she is most proud of being a wife of over fifty years to her best friend, George, a mother, a grandmother, and a great-grandmother. And one more thing… she is a leader who leads with tactical style!

Leadership Identity

When I was a young girl, I discovered a facet of personal power that made my mother cringe. I had a powerful voice. In fact, it was so powerful that everyone in our community knew when I was outside playing. It used to drive my mother wild when she heard me. I can still hear her voice.

"You are a lady and it's time you acted like one. I can hear your voice over every voice in the neighborhood! I don't want to hear your loud mouth when I open my windows and doors. Lord, what am I going to do with this child? You are a girl and it's time you sounded like one too." My actions frustrated her but it frustrated me that I had to do this "lady" thing she liked talking about.

I always felt that she wanted me to be more of a girly-girl. You know the dainty, quiet type with delicate manners, and gentle, flowing body movements. The type she could drape in ribbons and lace; the kind who sat and sipped tea from a rose-painted china cup. That was not me. My body movements were far from graceful, although I did try. I loved lace and ribbons, but I could only stand them for short periods of time.

My biggest challenge was when it came to playing because I loved being with boys. Most of the girls I knew were a bit too subdued for me. I preferred the invigorating thrill of battle over chattering about what dolls should wear. Most of the time I felt like an actor forced into a sad tragedy. This lady thing was pure torture for an active, battle-loving girl like me. Sitting and playing house was dull compared to a good game of war. The thrill of the hunt excited me.

The unbridled enthusiasm of boys exhilarated me and I wanted to be a part of all their drama. There was nothing more stimulating than hiding under a pile of leaves and then jumping out and capturing the enemy as they passed by my position. There was nothing that could compare with the thrill of jumping from a tree and rolling down a hill while carrying my camouflage. A green plastic machine gun was sheer bliss to me. My gun made a muffled, rattling sound. When I squeezed the trigger, the entire weapon vibrated and tickled my fingertips. It was sweet music to me.

The strategy, fighting, and winning—especially when defeat seemed inevitable—was riveting. I understood that although defeat might be in sight, victory could still throw a curve ball and help me slide into home base. It was not always the winning that gave me a thrill. It was the planning, plotting, and execution of a battle plan. It was like my very own private chess game.

I found new strength in my life as these gifts developed. I wanted to be a part of the action and could not without disobeying the adults in my life. Being female, playing quietly with dolls and disarmed from the battle was the purpose God created for me...or was it? To make matters more complicated, I did all this in a dress!

False reflections are not always bad.

Those times hold precious memories for me but as a girl, I always felt out of place. I lived in two worlds; the world of frills and lace and the world of guns and war.

Adults forced me to present a false reflection of my true self. When told to put down my weapon and pick up a doll, I had to find another way to be involved. Since I could no longer carry my weapon of choice, I had to learn to improvise.

The learning was not easy. I became a female volcano. I appeared calm on outside but there was a river of boiling, molten lava stirring within me. How did I keep from erupting? How did I release the pressure so the lava would not turn everything around me into a burning heap? I learned to be creative.

Instead of physically joining in the war games, I assessed the battlefield and shouted orders from the sidelines. The ones who objected were the boys who lost the battle. The boys who received the orders liked my contributions to their victory. They had no problem with my counsel as long as they won. I could see the victory before it happened and I quickly became the "accepted" female at neighborhood battlegrounds.

As I grew and matured, I soon came to understand that seeing the battleground strategies was a gift. I also encountered others who had this gift and joining forces helped me to win many battles. The opportunity to use the gift also served as a sharpening tool.

What I did not understand until years later was that I had the gift of tactical leadership. I could see when and how things needed to be done and then also see which gifts were necessary to fulfill a mission. Gender had little to do with the operation or execution of the gift.

I knew how to improvise in the midst of a battle and enjoyed watching others find their place of victory by using their gifts. I saw that no victory happened without a team effort. Through this process, I discovered the power of my God-given leadership identity. I am a tactical leader and improvising is my middle name!

6

The Creative Leader

No creativity, no mission.

If you scored more D's on the Leadership Style Inventory, you operate in the Creative Leadership style. You enjoy watching others interact and come up with their own way of doing things. You thrive while working behind the scenes and watching as others stand on foundations you and your team built. It might be a stage in a theatre production or a room decorated to perfection—both speak your leadership language. Your fingerprints are all over your work and no one has trouble recognizing your creative leadership signature.

You have no problem with others shining or taking the spotlight during a project. You understand that in order to get things done, everyone must play a role. Each person on your team must believe that their gifts are important. If they do not believe that they matter, then the project will suffer. You want only motivated and inspired people working with you because without inspiration, there will be no forward movement.

You never imitate anyone. You like being original and you like being you. Being unique has never been an issue for you. Because you are comfortable in your own skin, you dress the way you want and are not a slave to the corporate culture. Others may see this as a bit offbeat, but that does not matter to you. You live and work without excuse.

You avoid heated discussions. You leave those for more confrontational leadership styles. As a creative leader, you opt for staying in the background during leadership meetings. You prefer to spend time finding solutions instead of arguing.

You have the unique ability to see both sides of a disagreement and point out the good in both sides.

You discover solutions trapped in the fabric of conflict. Both sides usually have a piece of the puzzle so you try and listen objectively. While others jump into battle, you look for a way to acquire allies.

You enjoy reading reports from past leaders. You want to see what worked and how you can improve upon the past. There may be some interesting points that were unsuitable for past projects but will be a great fit for a present-day venture.

Finding a quiet place to read and sort through your day rejuvenates you. It gives you time to recharge your creative fire and prepare for the next day. Reflection also gives you the forum for developing new ways to do what you do. Quiet time is one of your best weapons against negative thoughts and feelings.

You read books that inspire and encourage you and you pass on information from those readings to your team members. Daily writing in your journal also helps to sort through your thoughts. Getting thoughts out of your head and onto paper gives you clarity and helps to generate ideas. Creative leadership is a gift. So cherish it and all it brings, because others need you and that gift to flourish.

Creative Leadership Strengths

Creativity and harmony flow throughout your leadership style. You and conflict cannot share the same space. When strife arises, you do one of two things. You leave the environment or you quickly try to find a way to help others see another way of doing things. You point out the strengths of both sides as well as the challenges they would face should they proceed in a different direction.

This does not always make you very popular. It may bother more demanding types who want you to take sides. The side they usually want you to take is their side. But for you, the only option is to do things the right way for the right purpose. You let everyone know that you are on the side of "right" and what best influences the mission and the organization. Everyone involved has something that will work to improve the situation. You just want everyone to contribute and have their say.

As a creative leader, you solicit input from your team members about how to handle a challenge so that they feel a sense of ownership to the process. You realize that not everyone wants ownership. There are some people who enjoy remaining on the fringes so they can complain or not take responsibility if something goes wrong. You have a gift for reaching this particular group of people. You help them to see the value of their input and also their value to the team and organization. Your love for the underdog always wins because you bring them to the table without much effort. In your creative leader way, you do something other leadership styles are unable to do. Because you understand what it feels like to be different, to feel disenfranchised, you can identify with those who feel unimportant. You help them to see their value and thus help them embrace the mission.

While you are not always in a position to make changes during disagreements, you can make suggestions for the best candidate for the job. You recommend your fellow tactical leader sister since she has the gift of forging ahead and placing the right people in the right positions to get things done even in the midst of conflict. You don't mind deferring to her because this is her specialized area of leadership.

When a new policy or procedure needs implementation, you have no problem supporting your sister activist leader. Your sister strategic leader wrote the policy and she stands waiting in the wings should anyone have questions. In true creative leadership style, you ensure that you and your team support their efforts for a smooth transition.

This is one of your greatest strengths—the ability to see the gifts of others and not be threatened by them when they use their gifts. Others may have challenges in this area, but not you. You want what is best for all concerned and when others can use their gifts, there is less conflict. For you, there is more than enough work to go around.

Dorcas

> There was a believer in Joppa named Tabitha (which in Greek is Dorcas). She was always doing kind things for others and helping the poor (Acts 9:36).

Sitting in the midst of a busy sewing circle, you see needles flying, scraps of fabric taking wing and fluttering through the air as women laugh and talk. Quilts, dresses, pants, and shirts all seem to miraculously appear in piles set aside for the poor. There is a jacket for an old man, sashes for the girls, and pants for the boys who help the fishermen. There are even sandals in all sizes. These things are for the people you serve. These are for the people of Joppa.

Your circle has a powerful purpose. Your sewing is more like a training session. You train the women of your city to sew and repair rapidly because the ranks of the poor swell daily. Not only do these women sew, but they also cook and house the city's poor. You are the leader of this circle and you coordinate everything, down to every needle and stitch.

You work without ceasing and because you focus on your mission, you ignore any minor pain or discomfort you feel. Exhaustion places his weary arms around you but you break his embrace with the whipping of your needle and by speeding up the pace, knowing that if you stop, someone will go without food, clothing, or shelter. This is your life's work and you want to make sure that the work never stops.

You get up this morning and prepare a small breakfast. As you sit down to eat, a subtle pain sends tremors through your chest. The pain tells you to stop and rest. You ignore it. It speaks again as it radiates down your arm and then sends a burning wave through your fingertips. You ignore the wave, hoping it will leave before the work begins. Today, you have a pile of broken sandals that need repair and working with leather requires special attention to detail.

You move on with your day, not giving it a second thought. Just as you sit down to your midday meal, your vision blurs and your legs turn into jelly. You try to stand but you are unable to move. With your last remaining ounce of strength, you force yourself up and the room violently spins and then everything goes black. Darkness ushers you into a place of quiet shadows and a strange peace holds your hand. You sleep.

In what seems like only a moment, a commanding masculine voice cuts through your sleep.

"Get up Tabitha!" The power of the voice is so strong that it reminds you of thunder. It shakes the darkness surrounding you as it gives way to the light. As you sit up on your bed, you see a flood of familiar faces. You see tears running, hands lifted, and your friends shouting and jumping. They all appear to be filled with some newfound joy which you do not understand. How could they be so excited about piles of worn clothing?

The man, whose name is Peter, tells you that you are awaking from a miracle. The spinning room, the pain in your chest, and the blurred vision carried to you the land of death. The people sent for Peter and he prayed and commanded you to return to the land of the living. You get to your feet, filled with a renewed sense of destiny and power. Your name is Tabitha and you are now what many would call a walking, talking miracle.

Tabitha, better known as Dorcas, was a creative leader who lived in the port city of Joppa. She had great compassion for the poor and worked tirelessly to help meet their needs. Because of her intensity, we can imagine that she ignored signs of stress. Those around her had more immediate needs. She could see the sick, the hungry, and the homeless. Their needs were ever before her as she walked the streets of Joppa.

When she arose from the dead, Tabitha worked with such tireless strength that her Creative leadership fire blazed a trail that is still burning today through the Dorcas Societies that provide clothing for the poor. Like you, her sister creative leader, Dorcas created an environment where others could work in harmony while serving those less fortunate.

Creative Leadership Challenges

As a leader, you solicit input from your team members about how to handle a challenge so that they feel a sense of ownership to the process. There are times when management may not see you as a team player because of your eclectic style, especially when a policy negatively impacts your team members. You have a knack for seeing how policies and procedures can hurt others and you don't mind sharing your opinion with management. Helping the underdog brings out the fight in you.

While many may see this as a personal strength, others may find it irritating. You would rather irritate someone than be accused of being uninvolved. Since you do not like conflict others may take your silence as a sign of not caring. Nothing could be further from the truth. You value the opinions of others even if you do not agree. You believe that others should and must offer their opinions so all can benefit. Once the opinions are out in the open, then and only then can everyone see all sides of an issue.

As a creative leader, you know that in the end, relationships are what keep a company strong. You work hard to help others see the value of becoming strong team members while still maintaining their individuality. It's challenging but you are up to the task, because you know how to creatively lead while making others feel important!

During conflict you usually wait to see if others can reach a conclusion before weighing in to help solve the problem. If you can't see resolution coming, you will wait for an opening and then give your opinion. Yours may not be an opinion they want to hear, especially since it will involve including others in the decision-making process.

You believe that everyone should have a seat at the table. The more information you gather, the better chances of solving a problem and helping the organization achieve its mission. You insist that everyone be heard, but there are those who may be unwilling to open their ears. They may see you as soft and someone who will not stand under pressure. You appear to take the side of the least resistance but that is far from the truth. You want to avoid future conflict but you also want what serves the greater good.

You always take up for the underdog and don't mind giving your opinion. When approached, you are always ready to defend your position with facts. You give solid examples of why management should listen and make changes.

You value all your team members; even those who differ from you. You will often hold your opinion and not offend others. This may not always be the best way to proceed since what you have to say may be the best solution. Your need to diffuse conflict should never outweigh the need for progress and organizational well-being.

You know that in the end, relationships are what really keep a company strong. Continue to work on expressing your opinion in support of your team, knowing that others may not always agree but they will respect you for speaking up.

As a creative leader, you work hard to help others see the value of becoming strong team members while still maintaining their individuality. It's challenging but you are up to the task because you know how to creatively lead while making others feel important!

Creating for the Creator

A painter paints because it is how she best expresses her passionate love for the Lord. A sculptor molds and shapes the clay because God created her hands for that purpose. A singer sings because her voice is an instrument of worship for the Most High. These expressions of creativity draw others closer to the Master Creator. In this life's race, we must pass on something to others. As a creative leader, you can pass on the fire of purpose to someone you love and watch as they draw closer to God. So take the opportunity to pass on destiny's baton and keep running, keep glowing, and keep creating!

Coco Chanel

> How many cares one loses when one decides not to be something but to be someone.

"Good morning, Giselle. What can we do for you today?" The shop owner smiled and her eyes danced with delight as she spoke with Giselle Moreau, one of her favorite customers. Mrs. Moreau was one of the most prominent women in Paris, and when she came into the shop she always purchased several items.

"What do you have in azure? My daughter is getting married and I just have to have one of your hats for the afternoon party. I need an azure dress for a garden party and everyone who is anyone will be there. I know I will stand out but it's not every day that one's only daughter gets married. As the mother of the bride, I must be…how do you say it again?"

"A girl should be two things: classy and fabulous," the two women said together as their laughter filled the shop. The shop owner pulled an azure hat from a box on the top tier of the shelving and her assistant approached with two azure dresses draped across her arms. As she walked to the fitting room, Giselle's eyes filled with soft mist of tears.

"You have done it again. I could not have found this anywhere else in Paris. I will be the envy of everyone there. Look at me. I love this! So brilliant, so simple, so elegant. *Merci beaucoup*, my dear friend. You make me look beautiful!"

"You are most welcome, Giselle. Your loving the clothes makes what I do joyful. Remember, fashion passes. Style remains. *Au revoir!*" As she spoke these words, this French shopkeeper had no idea that she was not just influencing the afternoon wedding party. She and her attitude towards fashion were destined to change the way women dressed all over the world. Coco Chanel was on her way to becoming one of the best known fashion designers the world has ever seen.

Coco Chanel was born in 1883, during a time when the voices of women were silenced unless they were projected or protected by a man. The woman who became known for class, elegance, and style started out in humble beginnings. Her mother died when she was six years old. Her father gave her and her four siblings to relatives.

She always had an artistic flair and once she became a young woman, she began designing simple hats. Male friends introduced her to women of high society and she and her hats became popular. She opened her first millinery shop in 1912 and was on the fast track to becoming a premier fashion designer in Paris.

She believed that women could look good and not suffer for it. She replaced the corset with comfortable unstructured lines. She was the first designer to use jersey knit from which she designed and made unstructured clothing. She believed that clothing should not hinder one's natural movements. Simple elegance flowed through her clothing and women loved it.

She replaced the rigid dresses of the era with comfort and casual elegance. Her fashion themes included uncomplicated suits and dresses, women's slacks, costume jewelry, purses with chain straps, and perfume. She introduced bell-bottoms, the pea jacket, and the box-cut bouclé jacket to women. She also introduced pajama styling and Chanel No. 5 perfume to the world.

She solved the mystery as to where women should wear perfume and introduced the Little Black Dress to her generation and to generations to come. There is hardly a woman in the Western world who does not understand the value of having a little black dress and pearls as an integral part of her wardrobe. Her fingerprints are embedded in the fashion world like no other designer, past or present.

Your creative leader sister Coco Chanel changed lives and blazed a trail of liberty for women that still burns brightly today. She creatively used her talents to not only clothe women but to show them that even the fashion industry can change the way others view life.

Creative Leadership Tips...

Don't allow others to stop your creative flow.

There are a few situations where your creativity stops flowing. You are a wellspring of creativity and even in the technical arena, creativity rules when you are in the leadership position. Although you can hold your own there are times when you need to rest. Instead of ignoring stress when he knocks at your door, take a deep breath and try to relax. There is no need to rush to show others that you are competent and can do your job. You can do whatever you decide to do but you still need balance.

Your creativity is the glue that will hold many projects together. If there is a problem that requires out-of-the-box thinking, you are just the person to solve it. In other words, others can see your gifts and when it comes to creativity, they will seek you out to ensure they have the right angle.

Feed your creative side by reading, writing, or doing something you really like. And make sure to spend time with other creative people. Whether it is crafting a new piece of jewelry, painting a landscape, singing a new song, or writing a letter, just stand in the river and let it flow!

Rest!

One of your biggest challenges is the ability to rest—especially when your creative juices are flowing. Sometimes rest means to stop. Stop working. Stop moving. Stop starting new projects. Stop trying to solve problems. Just stop. This is not an easy task, especially since creative minds don't stop running just because your body stops moving.

In order for you to walk in the fullness of your leadership style, you must rest. Resting helps to keep you focused. Resting helps to keep you sharp and ready to meet any challenges that happen during the day. When you have not rested, you can become irritable and cranky. You can lose focus and miss opportunities to share your creative fire.

Take small breaks. When you have trouble focusing, it is okay to stop and close your eyes for a few moments. Get up and move around. Get some fresh air. Remove yourself from the project for a few moments and just stand and take a deep breath. Get creative with how you take breaks! After all, you are a creative leader!

Make sure you have a safe place to vent.

Everyone needs a safe place to vent. Everyone needs a place where they can take off their shoes, let down their hair, and just allow freedom to have his way. That includes you.

Find a mentor or friend you trust. This should be someone who is far removed from your work or life challenges so that they can be objective. It should be someone who will not question the authenticity of your power because of your human emotions. In other words, it should be someone who understands that even powerful women need to vent and may say or do things when under pressure they would not normally do. It should also be someone who will not exploit your weaknesses.

Remember that you are a leader, and even the best of creative leaders need help and a safe place to express their feelings!

The Creative Leader and the Five Leadership Facets

Leadership Facet 1: Activation/Ignition

When a creative leader starts her ignition, people cannot always see it. Your inner fire does not always display itself to others once ignited. The conditions must be favorable to your creative style. You may appear to be <u>apathetic</u> to others but inside, you are gearing up to move. Background information revs your engine. History ignites you. You find old facts to ignite new projects. Why reinvent the wheel when all one has to do is see what worked and why it worked?

While everyone is arguing, you research. While others disagree, you look for cues to find harmony. In your eyes, there are always harmony cues if one would just stop and watch for them. These cues are the cornerstones that can be used as the foundation for future projects. Once you see the pattern, you can pull them together and help others to see how they can work together.

In order for there to be a perfect creative ignition, there must be harmony. There must be a purpose that feels right and looks right.

This is what ignites you. When you can see all the parts, you are able to flow and allow others to flow in their gifts.

Leadership Facet 2: Shifting into Gear/Direction

As a creative leader, you are one of the first people on a team to see the vision or the destination of your organization. While many may believe that there is only one way to do something or to get there, you believe that there are many ways to reach that goal.

If the plans call for everyone to stop and pick up supplies at a certain location, you and your team decide to get different supplies for a new route you've chosen. Instead of doing what others do, you chose a direction that helps members of your team to shine and enjoy the journey. You still end up at the same destination. You just chose a different path.

You also discover new and interesting facts you can share with the organization that may be needed for another journey. Being the creative genius you are, you know that others will take the trip just to see what you and your team have seen. It's just like you to start something new for others to stretch their creativity!

Leadership Facet 3: Inspiration (Motivation)/Acceleration

Because you are so creative, inspiration comes easily for you. Individuality and creativity go hand in hand and you help your team to see the beauty and power of that combination. Once everyone understands that they are important and that their gifts are necessary pieces of the puzzle, they will be able to accomplish what they set out to do.

When they understand that without them the mission would not look the same, run the same, or be the same, they can and will become inspired. Then they can see their part and move with inspiration's fire as they do what they've been called to do. And you are just the leader to light that fire and watch it glow!

Leadership Facet 4: Training and Development/Fueling

Training must be filled with necessary information but also fun! You create ways for your team members to use their gifts and incorporate the necessary skills to do their jobs.

When discussing how key components are necessary for a mission, you use a cooking class to show how key components are necessary facets of a mission. Using a standard recipe, you bake a cake and purposely forget to add the sugar. You also make a pot of coffee with only half of the needed amount.

You decorate the tables with china and make coffee. Your team enters the room expecting to taste a wonderful new dessert. But you have instead prepared a lesson in training for their afternoon delight. You invite them to have a cup of your "delicious" coffee and delectable cake.

Once the team tastes the unsweetened cake and drinks the weak coffee, you tell them how important it is to have all aspects of training in place to ensure that the work meets the standards. What better way to show how leaving out just one facet can impact an entire experience?

Leadership Facet 5: Rewards and Recognition/Maintenance

Rewards are a vital part of the creative leadership experience. You delight in recognizing your team and they know it. Like your sister the activist leader, you will create an award if the organization does not have one in place.

No work goes unrewarded. If you do happen to miss something it is only because no one brought it to your attention or because you were engrossed in another facet of the project. This is one of the reasons you give team members the freedom to help you see what you might miss. You expect them to point out the strengths of their fellow team members. This way recognition is a team effort and the responsibility of everyone. It also helps your team take ownership of the rewards process.

As a creative leader you know that recognizing others for a job well done is the only way to lead, and you do it with creative style!

Jessye Norman

> The very best thing that could happen to a voice, if it shows any promise at all, is when it is young to leave it alone and to let it develop quite naturally, and to let the person go on as long as possible with the sheer joy of singing.

I remember the first time I heard her voice. I wept. Tears streamed down my cheeks and wet the front of my fuchsia silk blouse. My shoulders shook as emotional tremors rippled down my back. I could barely stand. But there she was, singing with a voice that filled not only the arena stage, but my heart. She was singing so beautifully that the notes carried me back to my childhood dreams—my dreams of being an opera singer.

Teachers told me that there were no black opera stars and I had no way of knowing they were wrong. I was not reared in the African American community and at that time, knew little about my roots. My father was in the military and moved our family to Okinawa when I was only five years old. I never saw faces like my own when I was introduced to opera in elementary school. I only knew that when I heard Madam Butterfly, it touched a part of me I never knew existed. I wanted to be a part of it.

Throughout my school years, I knew that I had a strong voice but was told to tone it down. For years I sang a dull alto when all I could hear within me was a vibrant soprano. And now as I watched this woman singing on my television, I felt that I wanted to once again lift my voice and be heard. This powerful creative leader who touched my heart with her music was operatic soprano Jessye Norman.

One would just have to hear her sing to know why she is called one of the real divas of the operatic stage. There were no words to describe how the power of her vocal cords struck the very heart of me. There I was in my thirties and believing that I had missed my calling to sing opera. I could hardly believe it when I saw her on European television singing before thousands of people. Her presence captured the stage. Her voice filled the atmosphere like no voice I had ever heard.

Jessye Norman is one of the most celebrated opera artists in the world. Born and raised in Augusta, Georgia, she came from a musical family and grew up singing. She left her home in the South after winning a scholarship to Howard University in Washington, DC. As was fashionable in those days, she later moved to Europe to establish her career.

When asked to classify her voice, she refuses to do so. She has a wide vocal range from contralto to high soprano. She is also known for choosing to sing music that she believes best suits her voice and has been known to ignore the advice of producers and directors. She possesses an "imposing" stage presence and this, along with her magnificent voice, has ushered her into numerous starring roles in opera. She has even performed for royalty! In 1997, she made history and became the youngest recipient of a Kennedy Center Honor, making her a national treasure.

She is known as a trailblazer and has won the hearts of an international community. She has also influenced me. As a result of my viewing her on television, I rekindled my love for singing and toured Europe. I even performed "Stille Nacht" at the Beethovenhalle in Bonn, Germany, on the very stage where Beethoven performed.

Your creative leader sister Jessye Norman has used her creative gifts to open doors for herself and others...including me!

7

The Collaborative Leader

No relationship, no mission.

If you scored more E's on the Leadership Style Inventory, you operate in the Collaborative Leadership style. Others describe you as helpful, understanding, composed, and dependable. You are the cornerstone of your organization because it takes more than a crisis to shake you. You are calm under pressure, helpful when a need arises, understanding during a conflict, and dependable when there appears to be no support available.

You like celebrating others by hosting social events and dream of entertaining in an era gone by where lace and pearls ruled the day. Even your dress is understated elegance. Suits and simple blouses are your staples. With pen in hand, you are ready to tackle even the most detailed of projects because you are able to see what no one else sees. You know that ignored details can usually derail even the most finely tuned project.

You and your sister the strategic leader have much in common.

She is also a detail person—she develops the strategy and you see the holes and fill them. Working with her is like waltzing. You both dance to the same music. You just have to decide who is going to lead.

You are conservative in your actions and can usually spot where trouble will occur. Others also describe you as a team player. You shine when it comes to working with others for a common cause. You are a genius when it comes to making posters, developing surveys, and gathering data for a project. You thrive when working with a committee and love making collaborative decisions.

You do not allow your ego to play a role in what you do because you understand that the mission serves the greater good and is usually not about the individual. You do not enjoy working alone on the mission and have no problem helping others see where they fit while working on a project.

As a collaborative leader, you understand that laboring with others can be a joyful process as long as everyone understands the mission and they can see the part they have to play. You are just the woman to help them see how important they are to the overall project so that everything flows as it should.

Collaborative Leadership Strengths

Collaboration, or helping others work together, is the core of your leadership style. You are the consummate diplomat and you understand how to negotiate almost any situation, no matter how complex. You have the gift of bringing others together when nothing else has worked to bring them into agreement. You are an expert at creating connections and harmony between people within the organization.

You have your finger on the pulse of how others feel even when they do not express their feelings out loud. Your leadership style dream is to have complete harmony in the workplace. You want everyone to like and celebrate one another. Although you know this may never happen, you don't give up hope. You spread your essence of workplace fire around so everyone feels the warmth of its glow.

Your style focuses on the social and emotional needs of your team and places them over the organizational needs. You place the needs of your people before the needs of the organization because you realize that without the people, the organization cannot thrive. Once you have happy people, accomplishing a mission is the end result.

You are able to see both sides clearly of any conflict and do not mind working tirelessly to resolve issues. Others are surprised by your energy level. Although you appear to be calm and laid-back, your energy level soars when confronted with a situation where a resolution cannot be found. Your radar kicks in and you work with both sides to find a diplomatic solution.

Your ability to be objective is unlike that of any other leadership style. Clarity without judgment and collaboration without conflict are your leadership themes. You do not allow your personal feelings to impact negotiations. You are able to push past negative comments to "see through" hidden agendas of those at the table. Your work is your joy and the thrill of seeing others reach a joint agreement is reward enough for you. You take notes on what worked and keep a journal of the project, knowing that you will most likely need them in the future.

You are usually not a risk taker. You like working in situations that require low risk but offer high rewards. If anything requires a big risk, others can count you out. You like the "sure thing" in your life and workplace. You are laid-back and purposeful and will work until something is completed, which makes others see you as someone they can depend on in a crisis. This is one reason you work well with visionary leadership. You have no problem supporting visionaries and they need your stability to stay the course.

While working in a support position, you research, developing plans and strategies that will assist with the mission. You also have no problem flowing with other leadership styles. You don't mind taking a support position as long as it is a worthy cause. Being in the background is not something you mind.

When it comes to presenting a team position on an issue, you have no problem deferring this duty to a team member who is gifted at speaking. You write up and approve the information and then allow them to flow in their gifts. This is what a collaborative leader does. You allow others to flow so that collaboration can have her way.

You take the lead on social events. You never forget baby and bridal showers, birthdays, or promotions. You purchase a card and send around the envelope for others to participate in the life of their team members. You are the workplace glue that holds together the "human element" of the team and nothing says *collaboration* better than that!

Priscilla

Leader of the early church

> There he became acquainted with a Jew named Aquila, born in Pontus, who had recently arrived from Italy with his wife, Priscilla. They had left Italy when Claudius Caesar deported all Jews from Rome (Acts 18:2).

"I can hardly believe it but it finally happened. I knew it would come to this but I didn't expect it to happen so soon," she whispered as she folded her bed linens and placed them into a basket. Her hands shook as she sorted through the pile of clothing near her feet. She felt a sudden breeze run its fingers through her long, brown hair and then drape itself around her shoulders. It was a familiar visitor whose presence usually brought her joy, but today it could do nothing. Although it felt good, it was not good enough to paint its usual smile on her face. This had been her home for many years and now she had to walk away from all she knew.

"We will find another home; another place to begin again. This is not the first time we've had to start over. As long as we have each other, nothing is impossible," he said as he took her into his arms. A sigh escaped from her lips as she laid her head on his chest.

"Oh, Aquila, I know you are right. God is with us. Although I know this, I am still saddened by having to leave. I should be thankful that we are able to pack anything. Some of our neighbors were just thrown from their homes because Romans wanted to live in them. We are so blessed," Priscilla responded as she folded another scarf and gently placed it into the basket. She lifted her head and then took the back of her hand and dried the mist of tears that were beginning to wet her cheeks.

As she took a last, long look around the room, she saw many things she would have to leave behind: a table where she did her sewing, a chair where she sat and read each evening, and a large shelf where she and her husband kept their books. These things now belonged to the next residents of this dwelling place. These things, she thought, could be replaced.

Emperor Claudius had issued an edict for all Jews to immediately leave Rome. Priscilla and her husband Aquila were among them. Packing their belongings was difficult, but they knew that this was the start of a new beginning. Material things were unimportant. Many of their neighbors had been robbed and thrown into the streets. They lost everything, including their homes and all of their belongings. It was a blessing that she and her husband were able to pack without incident. Now, all they had to do was try and leave the city limits peacefully.

They decided to settle in Corinth. They did not know that there would be much work for them once they arrived. And they did not know that Priscilla was destined to become one of the most influential women of the New Testament church.

She and Aquila were early church leaders. The apostle Paul visited them many times and commended them and their church in his writings. They were tent makers, the same profession as Paul. They shared a profession and a faith, forming a collaboration that would last a lifetime and play an important role in the church.

We can imagine that this lovely Italian woman was important to the early church, especially since Paul typically mentioned her name before that of her husband in his writing. He also called her by the nickname of "Prisca," which signifies that they had a close relationship. This was unusual and shows that she played an important role in the early church movement.

What is most significant about Priscilla was her ability to work jointly with her husband in leadership and in teaching. One incident in the Bible (Acts 18:25-26) discusses how she and Aquila explained the Scriptures and brought clarity to Apollos, a prominent teacher of their day. This example of collaborative leadership is exactly what was needed for this critical time in church history.

When Paul left Corinth, they left with him and then lived in Ephesus. When Paul left Ephesus, he left the church there under their leadership. In his first letter to the Corinthians from Ephesus, he mentions Aquila and Priscilla and the church in their home. In 2 Timothy 4:19, Paul sent greetings to Prisca (who is again mentioned before her husband) and Aquila. Paul also mentions them with great affection again in Romans 16:4 where he talks about them risking their lives for his safety.

Once Emperor Claudius died, Priscilla and Aquila returned to Rome to continue their work. There is much evidence in Rome today that her work there made an impact. One of the oldest catacombs of Rome, the Coemeterium Priscilla, and a church on the

Aventine of Rome, the Titulus St. Prisca, were named for her. There are some Bible scholars who have even suggested that Priscilla was the author of Hebrews, since there is evidence it was not written by Paul, but by someone under his influence.

Your collaborative leader sister Priscilla mastered the art of collaboration during a time when women did not usually lead. She influenced not only God's people but also some of the most powerful men of her day. Like you, she understood that without relationships and collaboration there would be no mission.

Collaborative Leadership Challenges

You have the unique ability to bring harmony to the workplace. This sounds nice, but there are those who enjoy being unhappy and deal in negative whispers. Because your environment is your emotional thermometer, you try to make everyone cheerful. This could make you a target. When this happens, it hurts you so deeply that you may be tempted to call in sick just to avoid the conflict. Don't give your power away! Mean people exist and you cannot always escape. Stand your ground and don't give in to their pressure. Remember that there are some people who love being miserable and making others feel the same.

As a collaborative leader, you love to decorate your workspace with soft, floral patterns and watercolor pictures. These scenes make your world appear more peaceful. You have even been known to use rose-scented air freshener. Others may find your environment a bit over-the-top, but they are the first ones to enter your world when they face workplace challenges. The soft colors and the warm embrace of your world help them to feel welcome and relaxed.

Do not allow them to change you and how you operate. They need you to stay just as you are. There will always be negative people who want to keep the atmosphere polluted with negative energy.

You are a collaborative leader and you bring harmony to any negative environment. Just continue to be yourself! No one or nothing should be able to change that.

Most collaborative leaders avoid conflict. When others have a heated discussion, you will usually leave the room and wait for things to cool off. This is one of your challenges. You do not thrive in emotionally upsetting situations. Negative job performance meetings or team member disputes put you on guard. While you may be the team leader, open warfare is not where you thrive. You usually leave that to leaders with more confrontational styles, like your tactical leader sister. Learning to deal with these situations is challenging. You can take time and develop a strategy on how best to manage these situations by consulting with other leaders. Other leaders understand the need to confer and will be willing to assist you. All you need to do is ask. There will be times when they need your special gifts so make and keep those connections open.

You can also establish a committee of team members to assist you in making tough decisions that involve other team members. There is nothing wrong with obtaining assistance and feedback. Remember there is safety in the midst of counsel. You do not have to face things alone. Using this system also helps to develop other leaders within the ranks. Use your resources and they will serve you well. You should have little problem with this since you are the expert on collaboration!

> What are the best weapons to combat jealousy? Walk softly and carry a big smile. When you walk softly, you can walk in peace. There is nothing that can invade your peace because you control the atmosphere. When you smile, there is nothing that can erase it unless you allow sadness to overtake your attitude. You are in command. You are in control.

Marie Curie

"The soldiers in the field need X-ray equipment. We've got to help them! We are at war and they need help caring for our soldiers," she said. But no one would listen, so she took action. She did a quick study of radiology, anatomy, and automotive mechanics. She obtained X-ray equipment and generators and designed mobile radiology units for the field surgeons. They became known as *Petites Curies* (Little Curies).

During the first year of World War I, Marie Curie established twenty of these mobile units and installed two hundred radiological units at field hospitals. The estimated number of wounded soldiers served was well over one million. She also produced a hollowed-out needle which contained radon, derived from radium (taken from her own personal supply)—a colorless radioactive gas which was used for sterilizing infected tissue.

This was only one of Marie Curie's many achievements. She won Nobel prizes in two separate science categories—one in 1903 in Chemistry and the other in 1911 in Physics. Her gift of collaboration helped her to achieve this success.

Although she was born in Warsaw, Poland, physicist and chemist Marie Sklodowska-Curie did not achieve her success in her native land. She had to move to Paris, France, in order to pursue her dreams of becoming a recognized scientist. Once in Paris, she attended the Sorbonne and did most of her scientific research there. She understood that collaboration had to become an integral part of her life if she was going to succeed.

This belief led her to meet and then marry Pierre Curie. They were both intense researchers and scientists. Once married, they rarely left their laboratory and spent endless hours together. They shared interests and both loved long bicycle trips and traveling. These joint interests brought them even closer. In Pierre, Marie found a new love, a partner who shared the same interests, and a dependable scientific collaborator.

She became the first female professor at the Sorbonne (the University of Paris) and was the first woman to be entombed on her own merits in the Pantheon in Paris, an honor usually reserved only for men. She also founded the Curie Institutes in Paris and Warsaw. Both are still considered major medical research centers today.

She celebrated many achievements during her lifetime and nearly all were done while collaborating. Your collaborative leader sister Marie Curie made history by using her collaborative gifts to help the cause of science like no one before or since her time!

Collaborative Leadership Tips

Keep your sweet fragrance.

Don't allow the actions of others to make you bitter. Surround yourself with beauty. Listen to your favorite music. Hang your favorite paintings in your office. Create your world and then live in it without excuse.

You see and feel things that others don't perceive. Love yourself. Appreciate the beauty of who you are. Take care of yourself. Pamper yourself and protect that precious part of you. And remember... there is nothing wrong with you or your style!

Let no bitterness flow from your lips.

Your presence is like roses. You bring with you a sweet fragrance. This means that others may test you. They may say or do something against you to get you to say something unlike the real you. Do not allow them to steal your peace. Do not allow them to extract your joy. You are in complete control of yourself and your emotions. So stand firm on that!

Guard your heart and your lips. Remember, as a collaborative leader you are filled with harmony. When others reject your style, they are not rejecting you. They are rejecting one of the most precious gifts in the universe...peace!

Maintain your balance.

Make sure you maintain your balance by reading good books, taking time to reconnect with friends and family, and by leaving work at work. If you must bring work home, then have one day each week that belongs to you and only you. Work will still be there when you return. The reports will still be waiting when you need to complete them.

Your emotional health is critical and you must separate yourself from stress in order to maintain that collaborative style. You have a tendency to carry things emotionally. You are not strong enough to carry heavy people and situations on your own. Many people will want to pull on you because of your compassion and your love of harmony. Separate yourself!

Do what you can and leave the rest. This does not mean you should abandon anyone. It simply means that you must leave work and people issues at work so that they do not pollute your collaborative world and zap your energy!

The Collaborative Leader and the Five Leadership Facets

Leadership Facet 1: Activation/Ignition

When a collaborative leader starts her ignition, she usually begins with observation. You have the unique ability to see into the heart of a matter like no other leader. You work well with your sister creative leader. You do not mind giving her a portion of the project to oversee. This frees up your time and you can then focus on another facet of the mission.

When you all come back to the table, more work has been

accomplished because of your willingness to collaborate with other styles and types of leaders. Ignition has begun and the project gets done because you put aside your ego and instead opted for *relationship*. You created an environment for ignition where others could operate in their areas of expertise.

Leadership Facet 2: Shifting into Gear/Direction

As a collaborative leader, you believe there can be no shifting into gear without first activating the people. Relationships and environment are critical elements to ignition. Once you have your environment filled with positive attitudes and elements, you can activate your team. If your environment is not positive, then you will have mission failure. You cannot operate at your fullest potential without things being in place.

This is who you are and there is no need to apologize for what you need. You need what you need and you want what you want, and that's okay! Shifting into gear is only possible for the collaborative leader you when you have yourself together. So take care of *you* first. Then, and only then, can you shift and take care of others.

Leadership Facet 3: Inspiration (Motivation)/Acceleration

Relationship-building is in your blood. You understand the power of connection like perhaps no other leader. You are willing to compromise and let go of things that may not be critical to the mission in order to collaborate and then motivate others.

When they see that you are willing to work with them by sacrificing a part of what you want, then they are more willing to work with you on what you want. This inspires others because they want to work with you toward solutions. You and your collaborative leadership style serve as motivational tools to get the job done.

This leads to mission acceleration. Collaboration and motivation lead to inspiration—which leads to mission success! Not a bad combination for the collaborative leader!

Leadership Facet 4: Training and Development/Fueling

When it comes to training, you are just the woman to get things done. Again, your collaborative leadership gifts play a major role in helping your team reach their training goals. You activate the other leaders and allow them to cross-train. You believe in everyone knowing what the teams in other departments are doing. Learning never stops with your leadership style because without training and development, your team would fail. And that is something you work hard to avoid.

You encourage your team to develop this same attitude. It keeps them motivated to experience new things and makes them ready to capture new opportunities other teams may miss. It also keeps them mission-ready and excited about what can happen next.

And guess what? You are ready for anything that happens when training and development fuels your team.

Leadership Facet 5: Rewards and Recognition/Maintenance

For you, recognition and rewards are synonymous with relationship. One cannot exist without the other. Since you are a social thermometer, you can sense when dissatisfaction occurs. You ensure that everyone who deserves recognition receives it.

You appoint team members with the gift of exhortation to help with this critical mission facet. You understand that without recognition or appreciation, mission failure is inevitable. You work with other leaders to see what works for their team. You then take suggestions from your team on how they want to be recognized. If your organization has a recognitions program, you review it and even add to it to give it your own personal touches.

With your collaborative leadership style, you ensure that your team stays recognized so you all can take the next mountain!

Condoleeza Rice

> Education is transformational. It changes lives. That is why people work so hard to become educated and why education has always been the key to the American Dream, the force that erases arbitrary divisions of race and class and culture and unlocks every person's God-given potential.

When speaking of Condoleeza Rice, one could say many things. You can say that she was the first woman to serve as the National Security Advisor to an American president. One could also say that she served as the sixty-sixth Secretary of State under President George W. Bush—the first African American woman to do so. But one thing that is clear about her is her love for her country. She has been and remains a political force in our nation and has served in leadership positions usually held by men.

A staunch supporter of education, Ms. Rice has served as a professor of political science and as Provost at Stanford University. She also served on the National Security Council as an advisor to President George H.W. Bush during the end of the Soviet Union and Germany's reunification. While serving as secretary of state, she also served on the Millennium Challenge Corporation's board of directors. The mission of Millennium Challenge is to reduce international poverty through economic growth.

In 1993, when Ms. Rice was appointed as Stanford's Provost, she was responsible for managing the university's multi-billion dollar budget. There was a $20 million deficit at the time of her appointment. She promised that she would balance the budget within two years. Even though critics said it couldn't be done, Rice proved them wrong. Not only did she balance the budget, but she eliminated the deficit and the university had a record surplus of over $14.5 million. This helped to fuel her exposure which led her into the political arena.

After serving in the Bush administration, Rice returned to Stanford in 2009 and served as a political science professor. In 2010, she became a member of the Stanford School of Business and director for the Global Center for Business and Economy.

Ms. Rice has appeared four times on the Time 100, *Time* magazine's list of the world's 100 most influential people. This honor has only been bestowed on eight other people in the world. She was ranked the most powerful woman in the world by *Forbes* magazine in 2004 and 2005. In 2006, she was the number-two woman (following Angela Merkel, Chancellor of Germany).

On nearly every appointment and position she's held, your Collaborative leadership sister Condoleeza Rice has had to rely on her gift of diplomacy in order to achieve success. Like you, she understands that without relationship, there can be no collaboration. And without collaboration, there can be no mission success!

8

The Dramatic Leader

No glory, no mission.

If you scored more F's on the Leadership Style Inventory you operate in the Dramatic Leadership style. Dramatic is the perfect word to describe you and your leadership style. You love the look and feel of luxury in all areas, even in the workplace. Others describe you as enthusiastic, sympathetic, and gregarious. Because of your presence, they also describe you as influential, charismatic, and social.

You love recognition and you tend to decorate your office in lavish style. When someone enters your world, they usually don't want to leave unless they are more on the conservative side. One of your strongest needs is for your environment to reflect your personality.

Like your sister leaders, you believe that everyone has gifts to use and you want to include everyone involved. Because you like solid, dramatic solutions, you always want the best person for the job for optimal results. You do not have a problem letting someone know that you do not feel or believe that they are the right person for the job. The bottom line is that you want results. It is not about personality or whether you like someone. It is always about results.

You have a large presence and have no problem with making an entrance. You are a confident leader. Many mistake your confidence for arrogance, but they are mistaken. You understand your personal power better than most women and you are comfortable in your own skin and with your leadership abilities. You are so comfortable that you don't mind sharing the glory of victory with others. You know that without a strong team there can be no victory.

You work well when there is a cause. If there is not a degree of difficulty associated with a mission, then for you it is mundane. You love the feeling of just a little friction. It keeps things interesting.

You are dramatic in many ways other than your leadership style. Even your style of dress is dramatic. You love vibrant colors and are not afraid to show your femininity. You use accessories like a master fashion designer and they serve as image focal points for your style. Making an entrance is what you do best and you use your fashion styling to accentuate your leadership style.

You love the thrill of the hunt and take the lead on what others consider to be difficult projects. *The bigger the risk, the bigger the victory!* is your battle cry. You are fearless and that is unnerving to many. For you, it's a matter of knowing what you can do and understanding your limitations. If you have limited knowledge in an area, you seek out an expert. Hopefully, that person will be a member of your team. You always look to work with the best.

Your team members love working with you because they understand that each mission will be an adventure. You push them to their limit, which makes them better than when they started. Growth is what you seek. Excuses are not in your vocabulary. With you, everything is dramatic!

Dramatic Leadership Strengths

You feel comfortable projecting your personality and have no problem using it to obtain dramatic solutions. As a dramatic leader you also understand that not everyone will admire your style. That's okay with you because you are not out to please everyone. You are there to get the job done while connecting with people. You use your vibrant leadership personality to do just that.

You discover what makes your boss tick, and you tick with him or her. If she likes meetings, then you schedule meetings. If she likes teleconferences, then you work via teleconferences. If your boss likes lunches, then you get on her calendar for a regular lunch. Others may be threatened and wonder how you have the boss's ear. You know it's no secret.

You plan to rise in your organization and have no problem with personal power. You know that if you make a connection with decision makers, you will become a decision maker. And that is your ultimate goal: to influence the largest amount of people in the least amount of time. This is one of the trademarks of the dramatic leadership style.

You are a strong believer in teamwork. You believe that when you have a happy team, you will have a productive team. You will work tirelessly to ensure that your team members get what they need to do their jobs, even if you have to purchase the needed items. Your team members love you for it. They support your decisions and methods and take pride in being members of your team. They either love working with you or they leave. There is no in-between.

Your dramatic style does not lend itself to warm connections. Things are either hot or cold with you. You are the type of woman whom people either love or dislike. The people who dislike you usually cannot tell you why they dislike you. It's not because of something that you have said or done to them personally. It is just that your style may offend them.

Keep your head up. You know that things always change. People and seasons change and so will those who may dislike you. Because of your dramatic leadership style you may win them over, especially if you win a major victory for your organization. If they don't come to like you, they will respect you because you have no ill will toward others who do not understand or appreciate you or your style.

As far as you are concerned, they cannot stop progress as long as the Lord is on your side. He created you and your dramatic leadership style, so you look to Him to lead you so you can continue to lead others. And you do it with style!

The Queen of Sheba

> When the queen of Sheba heard of Solomon's fame, she came to Jerusalem to test him with hard questions. She arrived with a large group of attendants and a great caravan of camels loaded with spices, large quantities of gold, and precious jewels. When she met with Solomon, she talked with him about everything she had on her mind (2 Chronicles 9:1).

"Your majesty, all that we have seen we have told you. Everyone in his kingdom appears to be wealthy. Even the servants eat from golden plates and drink from golden goblets. We have never seen such wealth. Not only do they possess gold, but this king has great wisdom. It is unbelievable what we saw. He and his people have something different in their atmosphere. If we didn't know better, we would believe what we heard about their God," said the servant. His hands were shaking as he continued to describe what he experienced. "Yes, my Queen, he also…"

"Stop! I've heard enough," the queen interrupted. "Yours is one of numerous reports about this king of Israel. This Solomon must have a god at his disposal. I grow weary of hearing the reports. I shall travel to his kingdom and see for myself," she said as she motioned to her maidservant to draw near. There was an urgency in her voice and everyone surrounding her knew that she was about to do something that required their attention.

"Yes, my Queen," said the royal attendant as she bowed low. A smile flowed across her face as she lowered her head. She knew from experience that she was to be the bearer of some important news and could hardly wait to hear it, especially since the Queen appeared to be anxious. This always meant that something new was in the air.

"Give orders to my scribe. Send a message, along with a gift of ten talents of gold, to this King Solomon of Israel. Inform him that I, the Queen of Sheba, will visit him. Tell him that I am requesting an audience with him and I wish to see his kingdom for myself. Prepare and send the message and the gift now!"

The Queen of Sheba heard regular news of this king of Israel. Travelers, merchants, and even other kings had told her stories of his wealth, power, and majesty. She could take it no longer. She had to see everything for herself. Now she was preparing for this journey to Israel. Through the desert, sand dunes, mountains, and plains she would travel. None of this deterred her. She was a woman on a mission. This dramatic leader understood that there are times when you can take the word of another, but there also comes a time when you have to witness things for yourself. Today was that day. She beckoned for the traveler to tell her more.

"Well, your Majesty, when I visited his throne room, I witnessed how King Solomon settled disputes."

"Go on," said the queen.

"There were two women fighting over a child. Each woman said the child belonged to her. Each woman had a sad story and spoke of her love for this child. They told of how one child had died and that one of the women had exchanged the dead child for the living child. Now both women claimed the child as their own."

"What happened? What did he do?" asked the queen as she moved a little closer to hear the conclusion of the story.

"The king ordered his servant to bring the child to him. He told the women that he had the perfect solution to their dispute. He told them that his word was law and that once he made his decision, it would be final. Both women agreed." He took a deep breath before proceeding to the next part of the story.

"He ordered the servant to place the child at his feet. He drew his sword and then told the women that he would resolve the situation by taking his sword and cutting the living child in half. He then would give each woman half a child. One woman agreed. The other wept bitterly and begged him not to harm the child. She told him not to kill the child, but that she would rather give him up to the other woman. She gave up her claim so that the child could live. The king knew immediately that this was the true mother. He restored the child to her and the issue was resolved."

The queen could barely contain herself. She immediately left the throne room to prepare for her journey. She was also a ruler and understood that one must possess wisdom in order to rule effectively. She understood that with great power came great responsibility. She also knew with every fiber of her being that she needed to meet this King Solomon, because she believed that she had something to learn from him.

Great drama surrounded her journey. Over arduous terrain in the heat and sand, the queen and her caravan traveled until they reached Jerusalem. The Bible tells us in 1 Kings 10:2 that she came to Jerusalem with a very "large group of attendants and a great caravan of camels loaded with spices, large quantities of gold, and precious jewels." Your dramatic sister came prepared to see the great king and to pay homage with her gifts.

When she arrived in King Solomon's court, she was dressed in her finest robes and massaged with the finest oils from her kingdom.

She presented herself to Solomon in her most extravagant royal robes, her most brilliant jewels, and her most glorious crown. She was dramatic leadership at its finest. She was regal, dramatic, and impressive, even to men. They respected her not only as a monarch but appreciated her as a beautiful, powerful woman.

The Bible says she came to Solomon and spoke with him about all that was in her heart. He answered all her questions above and beyond her satisfaction. In 2 Chronicles 9:5-9 she exclaims,

> "Everything I heard in my country about your achieve-ments and wisdom is true! I didn't believe what was said until I arrived here and saw it with my own eyes. In fact, I had not heard the half of your great wisdom! It is far beyond what I was told. How happy your people must be! What a privilege for your officials to stand here day after day, listening to your wisdom! Praise the LORD your God, who delights in you and has placed you on the throne as king to rule for him. Because God loves Israel and desires this kingdom to last forever, he has made you king over them so you can rule with justice and righteousness." Then she gave the king a gift of 9,000 pounds of gold, great quantities of spices, and precious jewels. Never before had there been spices as fine as those the queen of Sheba gave to King Solomon.

She blessed the name of the Lord, his God for making Solomon king over Israel. This is significant, since Sheba was an idolatrous country.

Her visit was historical not only because she was a woman, but because of her dramatic leadership style. Her visit was the beginning of commercial trade and growth for Israel and a new connection for Sheba.

Like you, her dramatic leadership sister, the Queen of Sheba made her entrance and changed history. She listened to others but also insisted that she see things for herself. Nothing could stop her—not wind, sand, harsh terrain, or heat. She went before the king and the rest, they say, is history!

Dramatic Leadership Challenges

Drama can surround you and your leadership style. If you don't take care of yourself, you could become unbalanced. When this happens, you could become judgmental.

Dramatic leaders may misjudge the actions of others. If you hear someone criticizing the company, you may believe that the person is not a loyal employee. It may be that the person was just having a bad day and their problem was not actually with the job. When you see someone mistreat another person, you could record this error in judgment as the permanent character trait of the person involved. Watch and learn. People are not perfect and tend to bring their personal issues to work. Take a deep breath, watch, and wait before you say or do anything.

Make sure you give credit where credit is due. There are times when dramatic leaders tend to overlook the work of others. They don't always share the recognition with team members. Before taking credit for work, make sure that you check the contributions of others. Ask questions. Stop and check your notes. Hold a meeting with your team when news of the recognition reaches you. The last thing you need is to overlook someone for a job well done. This could cause unnecessary strife which erodes morale and damages the mission.

You have a unique style which does not change when you lose or gain weight, change jobs, or get married or divorced. God placed it inside you at birth and you cannot reject it even when you try not to be you. That means that you cannot deny it. Because it is a God-given gift, you can walk without excuse in the beauty of your dramatic leadership style. And as you do, just remember to take care of yourself and observe how you impact others.

> Competent leaders understand the diamond principle. They know that it takes time and the pressure of the earth to turn a piece of coal into a diamond. They also understand that in order for there to be a great reward, they must first be willing to make a great sacrifice.

Queen Elizabeth I

> Though the sex to which I belong is considered weak you will nevertheless find me a rock that bends to no wind.

The rise to power can be arduous, but one female monarch stands as an example to women around the world. When one thinks of women who changed the way the world saw female rulers, Queen Elizabeth I will certainly be at the top of that list.

She was the daughter of King Henry VIII. Her mother, Anne Boleyn, was executed when she two and a half years old. She had the fortitude and boldness of her father and the tenacity of her mother. She became one of the most powerful rulers in Europe when war was on the daily menu of most countries.

History sometimes refers to her as the Virgin Queen. She was the fifth and last ruler of the Tudor dynasty. She relied heavily on a group of trusted advisers, Williams Cecil and Baron Burghley. One of her initial moves as monarch was the establishment of the English Protestant church, of which she became the Supreme Governor. This soon evolved into what is known today as the Church of England.

Those in the court expected Elizabeth to produce an heir to continue the Tudor line. She never did, although she did have numerous men vying for affections. Elizabeth was more moderate than her father and half-siblings and one of her famous sayings was *video et taceo* ("I see, and say nothing").

In 1570, the pope declared her illegitimate and sent word to her subjects that they should no longer honor her. Because of this action, there were several attempts on her life. All assassination attempts failed with the help of her ministers' secret service.

Elizabeth was guarded in foreign affairs, especially when dealing with the major powers of France and Spain. The talk of war filled her reign and other countries challenged her because of her gender. She halfheartedly supported poorly financed military campaigns in the Netherlands, France, and Ireland. This did nothing but make her appear more vulnerable to other European nations. Spain decided to invade and conquer England in 1588, but they suffered a humiliating defeat. The defeat of the Spanish Armada is viewed as one of the greatest victories in English history.

Queen Elizabeth was known as a strong, charismatic ruler and a survivor at a time when governments and monarchies experienced internal drama that threatened their thrones. Many of these kingdoms knew that they could fall at a moment's notice, but not Elizabeth's.

Your sister dramatic leader Queen Elizabeth I survived every attempt to take her life and throne. She made history as one of the most powerful women to ever rule a nation.

Dramatic Leadership Tips...

Continue to be you.

There is nothing more frustrating than having to hide your true identity. Any dramatic leader knows this. Your dramatic leadership style shines through for the entire world to see. You are a true woman of identity. You keep it real. Don't let anyone take that from you.

There will be others who accuse you of things you know you didn't do. Your biggest hope is that those who know you will be able to identify your work. They will be able to tell if a story is a counterfeit. You understand that you are dramatic and stories come with the territory.

Your style, although dramatic, is a gift. Don't ever doubt that. The enemy wants nothing more than for you to shut yourself down and stifle your style. God created you to "shake things up" and to keep others moving. Your very footsteps create thunder so loud that the enemy hates for you to get up in the morning. So, my sister, keep doing what you do and don't hold back on your dramatic style! We need it!

Remember that others don't always agree with your methods.

While you may mean well, others may see some of your methods as deceptive and manipulative. They do not understand that you watch and study others. You want to make sure that everyone is comfortable in doing their jobs. You are also aware of how you influence others. You try to gauge your actions so that others will not become threatened. Although many do become threatened, you try and manage that aspect as best as you can. When you do things that please your boss, remember that jealousy can follow.

Since you have a gift for connecting with upper management, others may see you as a social climber. You are comfortable with those in power and understand that they are just people like you. And you treat them accordingly, which most of them appreciate. You have no problem telling management the truth about workplace issues and although many executives may not like what you have to say, they respect that you do have the courage to say it. So when they want the truth, they call on you to present it.

Continue to stand firm in the beauty and power of your leadership style and nothing can change you. God created you for your mission, so do it to the best of your ability and leave the rest to Him. Connect with management and show others that power and influence are a necessary part of connecting at work and getting the job done. Doing it as a dramatic leader is what you do best, so do it!

Don't forget to take care of yourself.

This is an area where you may fall short and you should use caution. You are so mission-focused that you have difficulty saying no. You can take on too much work and then stress begins to take its toll on you, your attitude, and your body.

Rest and exercise are necessary for your leadership style. Your presence is larger than life and all eyes are on you. If you succeed, you succeed big. If you fail, you fail big. So stop and take a necessary stress break. Have soft music in your office. Try herbal tea instead of coffee. Instead of scheduling numerous working lunches, take walks. Take a bubble bath at least once per week. Surround the tub with scented candles and just relax. Have a pedicure and manicure regularly.

Stop trying to do it yourself. Allow someone else the honor of serving you since you serve so many others. Care for yourself because you need your strength and energy to be your dramatic best!

The Dramatic Leader and the Five Leadership Facets

Leadership Facet 1: Activation/Ignition

When a dramatic leader starts her engines, ignition is obvious. You jump into action and inform your team of the project. You fully expect everyone to notice where they fit on the project team because they should already be aware of how to use their gifts. They should already be prepared for this moment.

You start discussions and expect answers. You want results as soon as you can get them and you let your team know that ignition is starting and you will be shifting into gear to start the journey. You appoint those who will take the lead to start the process. You give instructions on how things should flow and you expect your instructions to be followed to the letter.

You appoint team members who enjoy research to begin researching the best way to begin. You activate those who can access resources to begin gathering what you need to begin the work. Every team member has a job and knows and understands their role in achieving success.

Leadership Facet 2: Shifting into Gear/Direction

Shifting into gear is easy for you and your team because you keep everyone mission-ready. You drill your team on what to do and how to do it on a weekly basis. All you have to do is hit cruise control. Everyone on your team understands where they need to be and how they need to operate in order for the team to be productive.

Your administrative staff readies themselves to manage the paper or correspondence trail. Your operations staff meets to design the process. You may have several scenarios you can use and they must ascertain which one will work for a particular project. Your social media staff readies itself to generate any necessary media should the need arise. You and your leaders then place any new or extra staff in place before the project starts. Once you have everything in place, you shift into gear, ready for the next move.

Leadership Facet 3: Inspiration (Motivation)/Acceleration

Most dramatic leaders operate in the gift of exhortation and don't mind using it. Since you always do things in a big way, this area is easy for you. You just give your staff what you would expect. You love seeing them compete and grow together. You let them know that you expect them to be promoted and to outgrow your department.

It gives you a thrill to watch another member of your team receive a promotion because you know you prepared them for it. You like having a reputation for inspiring your team to success and the best way to do this is to continuously exhort and encourage them to excel. It is the only way to go for a dramatic leader!

Leadership Facet 4: Training and Development/Fueling

Training is an ongoing process in the dramatic leadership camp. You appoint mentors for those who are new to your team. You have already trained your team members to be leaders and expect to see the leadership process in action, even during a mission. For you, this is the only real way to assess if your training system is working.

You have systems in place for each leg of the project. You use the same format and after the project is over, you and your team perform an assessment to ensure that your system remains sound. During this time you can also adjust the system for necessary improvements.

In dramatic style, you have training as a constant facet of daily operations. It's the only way you operate.

Leadership Facet 5: Rewards and Recognition/Maintenance

You do everything in a big way, including recognizing staff for a job well done. You love celebrations and have a special staff member appointed to manage this leadership facet. You use the available organizational recognition system and add your own touches. Your staff always enjoys these sessions because you have new and different ideas each time. You try and outdo what you did in previous celebrations to keep things interesting and fun.

Your team members appreciate the time you take to ensure they receive their recognition. It is seldom that you overlook someone but it does happen. This is one of reasons you have a special assistant to help in this area. The last thing you want to do is exclude someone from this special process. To you, recognition is one of the most critical facets of good team management.

Charlayne Hunter-Gault

> If people are informed they will do the right thing. It's when they are not informed that they become hostages to prejudice.

When thinking about a woman who displays the dramatic leadership style for today's woman, Charlayne Hunter-Gault comes to mind. Born into a military family and serving as a foreign correspondent, she was destined to become a trailblazer for women.

In 1963, she did something few women with her background had done. She attended the University of Georgia and fell in love with Walter Stovall. She and Walter married in March of that year in Georgia. They then went to Detroit and in June of that same year married again for fear that the marriage would be deemed illegal in the South because of the laws. Why might their marriage have been illegal? Charlayne is African-American and Walter is White.

When news of the marriage reached the Governor's office, he called it a "shame and disgrace." The Attorney General considered prosecuting the mixed-race couple under Georgia law. According to news reports, both sets of parents were against the marriage because of race.

The couple divorced in 1972. Years later, Hunter-Gault gave a speech at the university in which she praised Stovall, who, she said, "unhesitatingly jumped into my boat with me. He gave up going to movies because he knew I couldn't get a seat in the segregated theaters. He gave up going to the Varsity because he knew they would not serve me. We married, despite the uproar we knew it would cause, because we loved each other." Shortly after their marriage,

Stovall was quoted as saying, "We are two young people who found ourselves in love and did what we feel is required of people when they are in love and want to spend the rest of their lives together. We got married." The couple has one daughter, Susan Stovall, a singer.

This was not the first time Hunter-Gault had made a public move against racism. In 1961, she and Hamilton Holmes were the first African-American students to enroll at the University of Georgia. She graduated in 1963.

She joined the investigative news team at WRC-TV in Washington, DC, where she also anchored the news in 1967. She later joined the New York Times as a metropolitan reporter where she specialized in the urban African-American community. This prepared her for next assignment with *The MacNeil/Lehrer Report* in 1978 where she became the *The NewsHour's* national correspondent in 1983. In 1997, she left *The NewsHour with Jim Lehrer* and began work in Johannesburg, South Africa, as National Public Radio's chief correspondent in Africa. She served in that position until 1999, then left to serve as CNN Johannesburg's bureau chief and correspondent.

While associated with *The NewsHour* she won two Emmys and a Peabody for excellence in broadcast journalism for her work on "Apartheid's People," a NewsHour series on South Africa. The National Association of Black Journalists named her the Journalist of the Year in 1986. In 1990, she won the Sidney Hillman Award, the Good Housekeeping Broadcast Personality of the Year Award, the American Women in Radio and Television Award, and two awards from the Corporation for Public Broadcasting for excellence in local programming.

In 1992, she wrote *In My Place,* a memoir about her experiences at the University of Georgia. Your dramatic leadership sister won awards for her work and operated with such flair that she left her mark on international journalism. She stepped across invisible lines, lived her life out loud, and made history.

9

Leading with Style

When you think about what women of the past have faced, one can only pause and wonder how they made it. Parting seas, advancing armies, breaking the law, and rising from the dead; nothing could keep them down because these girls had guts! They had the boldness to stand alongside their brothers and write history. They had the audacity to grasp their God-given purpose and face adversity.

They each brought something different to destiny's table that helped to serve a meal for the ages. One had songs that erased fear as her people crossed the Red Sea. One embraced warfare and helped her country become victorious in battle. Another draped herself in feminine courage and so mesmerized a king that he offered her up to half of his kingdom. After being raised from the dead, another woman started a sewing society that spread through the ages and still serves the poor of today.

These women are entrepreneurs, educators, journalists, rulers, and Nobel Prize winners. They did things that made headlines and broke barriers that others said they could never break. They are mothers, sisters, and friends. They are women we know and love and they opened the doors to the future for us to step through without fear.

They all had the ability to seize the moment and change the atmosphere. They all led. Not one stepped back from her duty. Not one even stopped to think about herself. Each woman only had the mission and the people she served in her radar. Now, imagine all the emotions, faith, strength, and courage it took to accomplish missions, especially during the times in which they lived. Their acts are synonymous with power and action and have even crossed gender lines as testaments of courage. These women all stepped into destiny and led with style.

The Daughters of Zelophehad

The girls knew their power!

One day a petition was presented by the daughters of Zelophehad—Mahlah, Noah, Hoglah, Milcah, and Tirzah. Their father, Zelophehad, was a descendant of Hepher son of Gilead, son of Makir, son of Manasseh, son of Joseph. These women stood before Moses, Eleazar the priest, the tribal leaders, and the entire community at the entrance of the Tabernacle. "Our father died in the wilderness," they said. "He was not among Korah's followers, who rebelled against the Lord; he died because of his own sin. But he had no sons. Why should the name of our father disappear from his clan just because he had no sons? Give us property along with the rest of our relatives" (Numbers 27:1-4).

When I think of what collaboration looks like for women in leadership, the five daughters of the Zelophehad always come to mind. They had no male relatives and these girls understood that there was property to be had. During the time they lived, property passed from father to son. If there was no son, it went to another male relative. These women had no close living male relative. What's interesting is that their father knew he had no close male relatives and yet he made no appeal to Moses or the elders regarding the care of his daughters. If he had made a request, it certainly would have been recorded. I believe that God allowed things to happen just as they did as an encouragement to His present-day female leaders.

We can imagine that these women were initially frightened about the prospect of coming before Moses and the elders. They were on the verge of being homeless and living with no inheritance. They knew that if they were going to make an appeal, they had to be in agreement. Maybe Mahlah, whose name means *sickness*, did not want to go. I can imagine that her sisters had to coax her. Noah, whose name means *movement*, might have come up with the plan. She had the plan and was ready to execute it without delay. Hoglah, whose name means *partridge*, probably just wanted to fly away but went along with the others anyway because she had no place to land if she did choose to fly away. Milcah, whose name means *queen*, might have told her sisters that they deserved the possession and she would be willing to lead the discussion should the need arise. Tirzah, whose name means *delightful*, might have been in agreement with whatever her sisters decided. I imagine that she was delighted to go along because she did not want to live without security.

These women approached Moses in feminine unity. In Numbers 27:5-8, we see how Moses brought their cause or request before God. God told Moses to give them their portion.

What message is in their story for us? This tells us that as women, we need one another when we make our request to God. If we are to find favor, we need to link arms with our sisters and make our requests. We no longer have to go before Moses because we have a Great High Priest who shed His blood to give us this privilege. We can come boldly before the throne of grace and make our requests known to our God.

I believe the Lord gave the daughters of Zelophehad to us as an example of how we should collaborate. There is power in our ranks…if we stick together. We must learn to walk in unity with other women, whether we like them or not (or whether they like us or not). If your sister cannot walk, reach down and help her stand. If she cannot see, then help guide her to the paths of righteousness for His name's sake. If she cannot hear, then whisper His word into her ears until she hears that still, small voice on her own. If she is hurting, then hold her in your arms as the gentleness of His love flows through you. If she is bleeding, then dress her wounds with the power of His healing. If she is standing, walking, talking, moving and loving, then link arms with her and lead others into His presence.

We must learn to act as one unit. Our Father will move for us when He sees our singleness of purpose. We are His daughters and there is nothing that can change that.

There can be no victory without warfare. When we learn the beauty of feminine power and see it at work, we can see how wonderful it is to be a woman leader of today. We can make wise choices and use our power for good and not for evil. So like the daughters of Zelophehad, we can see that collaboration among women leaders is a beautiful thing.

The Feminine Facet of the Body of Christ

The Proverbs 31 Woman

> There are many virtuous and capable women in the world, but you surpass them all! (Proverbs 31:29).

Many years ago, I wrote a book entitled *Daughters of the King*. After writing the book and discovering my image type, the Lord instructed me to read Proverbs 31 and the verses on the Virtuous

Woman. She was the last person I wanted to think about. I had finally arrived at a place where I liked myself. I could not understand why God would snatch me from my safe house of self-acceptance. Why would that still, small voice thunder the request to study this creature of perfection? I did not like this woman who did not seem to eat, sleep, or even take time to use the bathroom!

I heard messages on this woman and each time I left church services feeling inadequate. I was feeling good about my identity for the first time in my life. I also had experienced enough defeat to last for a lifetime and the Proverbs 31 Woman brought me little comfort.

I made up my mind that these verses of Scripture simply did not apply to me, so I could just "skip over" them and act as if they never existed. You see, I felt that it was impossible for me to live up to the standards of the virtuous woman. Why try when you know something is impossible?

But still I cringed while sitting in church nearly every Mother's Day. The pastor would talk about his dear, old mother. The Scripture text he used? Proverbs 31. It always seemed odd to me that this woman was the star of the show every Mother's Day. It was as if every pastor used this woman as an example as they described feminine perfection. So knowing I was not perfect, I ran because of the Proverbs 31 Woman.

I just could not see how any woman in her right mind could even try to live up to that image. I was not the stay-at-home type. I did not enjoy cooking, cleaning, washing, or taking care of children. I also knew that if I let any of the other women know how I felt, they would heap condemnation's heavy stones on my head. I was living a lie. I was a good Christian girl and wanted everyone else to think so too. Telling the truth about this woman was certain social "death" in the church.

Those verses were for other women. You know—the ones who like to cook, clean, wash, dry, sit, dance, jump, skip, and work inside and outside the home. The ones who serve on every committee, coordinate all activities, and still have happy marriages and healthy, clean children. They arrive at church on time with their perfect families in their perfect clothing riding in their perfect cars. I had nothing in common with these women who appeared to have this Proverbs 31 Woman image together.

Realizing that I could experience no peace until I responded to God, I started reading about the Proverbs 31 woman. After reading those verses, I felt stripped of all accomplishment. Whenever I read about this woman, my faults seemed like sky scraping, jagged mountain peaks. I felt as if I was standing at the foot of a cliff without any climbing equipment. I could see an avalanche of self-pity begin its thunderous fall upon my head. As it approached, I stood frozen in time and cried out, but no one heard me—no one but this perfect sister of mine.

I heard her voice saying, "If your lamp had not gone out at night, you could have seen that the way was not safe and avoided the avalanche. If you had considered a field and bought it, you would not have had time to be standing at the foot of a mountain anyway. If strength and honor were your clothing, you would not have suffered from the coldness of a low self-image." As I struggled to catch my breath, she continued spouting out verses from Proverbs 31. When the avalanche finally reached me, it ripped away the core of my femininity and buried me under a ton of self-doubt and self-pity.

As I read about this I questioned my identity. From where I sat, the enemy had stepped in and fooled me into taking this self-defeating journey. Knowing how the Lord loves a good joke, I asked if He was serious. Was it His desire that this Proverbs 31 Woman serve as my role model?

Before we go any further, I hope you understand this was a revelation God shared with me. It made so much sense that I wanted to share it with you. It is such a simple truth, yet, because of its simplicity, there may be things that could block what I believe God wants me to share. I know because I wrestled when the Lord first gave this to me.

The first thing God told me was that alone, I would never achieve what was written about the Proverbs 31 woman. Of course, I already knew that before I could ask.

As the Holy Spirit gave me this marvelous revelation, He continued speaking and I heard the word *unity*. He said that there must always be unity in all God's work. Even when the Lord brings destruction, He always works in unity. There is never chaos. He uses precision in all things.

Let me ask a few questions. Would you agree that both men and women are components of the body of Christ? Would you also agree that men and women have obvious differences? If you agree, then you must also realize that our Creator knows about these differences. He created everything, including man and womankind, with precision and balance. He not only created us, but He also provided the road map and instructions for us to walk life's road in unity. Our sister the Proverbs 31 Woman is our example of feminine excellence.

One Body with Many Parts

The human body has many parts, but the many parts make up one whole body. So it is with the body of Christ. Some of us are Jews, some are Gentiles, some are slaves, and some are free. But we have all been baptized into one body by one Spirit, and we all share the same Spirit. Yes, the body has many different parts, not just one part. If the foot says, "I am not a part of the body because I am not a hand," that does not make it any less a part of the body. And if the ear says, "I am not part of the body because I am not an eye," would that make it any less a part of the body? If the whole body were an eye, how would you hear? Or if your whole body were an ear, how would you smell anything? But our bodies have many parts, and God has put each part just where he wants it. How strange a body would be if it had only one part! Yes, there are many parts, but only one body. The eye can never say to the hand, "I don't need you." The head can't say to the feet, "I don't need you." In fact, some parts of the body that seem weakest and least important are actually the most necessary. And the parts we regard as less honorable are those we clothe with the greatest care. So we carefully protect those parts that should not be seen, while the more honorable parts do not require this special care. So God has put the body together such that extra honor and care are given to those parts that have less dignity. This makes for harmony among the members, so that all the members care for each other. If one part suffers, all the parts suffer with it, and if one part is honored, all the parts are glad. All of you together are Christ's body, and each of you is a part of it (1 Corinthians 12:12-27):

A Seven-Faceted Diamond

Now these are the gifts Christ gave to the church: the apostles, the prophets, the evangelists, and the pastors and teachers. Their responsibility is to equip God's people to do his work and build up the church, the body of Christ. This will continue until we all come to such unity in our faith and knowledge of God's Son that we will be mature in the Lord, measuring up to the full and complete standard of Christ (Ephesians 4:11-13).

Here is the part of the revelation that may challenge your present way of thinking. The Lord explained that the body of Christ contains seven facets. He said the body is like a seven-faceted diamond. He revealed those seven facets to me. These are:

- apostles
- prophets
- evangelists
- pastors
- teachers
- male
- female

The body of Christ, like a diamond, contains beautiful facets that make it a brilliant, beautiful gem. Just as a diamond delights the eye of man and woman, the facets of the body of Christ delight the eye and heart of our Lord. Together, we make up the Lord's special treasure!

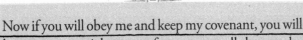

Now if you will obey me and keep my covenant, you will be my own special treasure from among all the peoples on earth; for all the earth belongs to me (Exodus 19:5).

The feminine facet shines brightest when women work together in unity and glorify Him. This treasure, which resides within us, glows in the eyes of our God. The harder we work toward this goal, the brighter the treasure shines. As we work together, rough edges get scraped off and polished. The feminine facet of the body of Christ then radiates more intensely with His beauty.

The Proverbs 31 Woman is what our Lord sees when the feminine facet of the body of Christ works together in unity, when women come together to work for a corporate cause. No woman is more important than another, and each woman is interdependent upon the other as she does what she is called to do for God. We must work together for those beautiful verses to have the full impact our

Father intended. We shine brilliantly when we work together as one for the One who created us.

> We now have this light shining in our hearts, but we ourselves are like fragile clay jars containing this great treasure. This makes it clear that our great power is from God, not from ourselves (2 Corinthians 4:7).

Could it be that we have been so busy trying to be all things to all people that we missed the whole point of the Proverbs 31 Woman? Could it be that every woman who patterned her life after this woman had the correct information, but the incorrect interpretation? I can only say that I've seen generations of women almost kill themselves trying to be more like Sister Proverbs.

Women have gotten up out of sick beds to escape condemnation's haunting laughter. Women have neglected themselves because of unspoken standards imposed upon them by other women, both past and present. They worked from sunup until sundown, so why shouldn't we?

They had babies and got up from childbirth's table and cleaned their houses, cooked their evening meals, and took care of others with a nursing child on each breast. So why should it be any different for us? These questions torment us as voices from past generations throw criticism's stones of judgment, blocking our paths toward wholeness.

I believe what the Holy Spirit says. I believe that the Proverbs 31 Woman is what our Lord wants to see when He looks at us. We shine brilliantly when we work together as one for the One who created us.

Using the six leadership styles from the previous chapters as a guide, you will be able to see the beauty of what He showed me. After making this discovery, I realized that I could relax and enjoy my life more. I realized that I had to learn to work with other women to get this thing right with God. He broke it down so that even I could understand it.

Each leadership style represents a feminine body part and performs special functions. They are as follows: The activist leader represents the hands, the strategic leader represents the head, the tactical leader represents the neck and shoulders, the creative leader represents the arms and back, the collaborative leader represents the heart and torso, and the dramatic leader represents the hips and legs. The feet rest on God's Word, which serves as our foundation.

If we want to walk in excellence as the feminine facet, we must stand on God's Word and allow Him to order our footsteps. That's what it's going to take because if we could do it on our own, we would already be doing it! His Word destroys yokes that block liberty from embracing us.

Most women do not have a perfect figure. We reach for an all-in-one body shaper which supports and lifts our hanging parts. Just as the body shaper keeps our body parts in place under our clothing, so the Father keeps the body parts of the feminine facet in place. He is the great All in One. He keeps the hands attached to the arms, keeps the neck and shoulders in line, supports the head, and moves the arms. He gives strength to the back and keeps the chest and torso aligned to support the neck and shoulders. He aligns the hips and legs so they stay grounded on the Word, for…

> Your word is a lamp to guide my feet and a light for my path (Psalm 119:105).

Join me as we discover a new way of seeing the Proverbs 31 Woman and see the beauty of your leadership style in action. As you read this revelation, I pray that liberty will sing your song. God specializes in making roads in your wilderness and rivers in your desert. He said that He would do a new thing and now it shall spring forth!

For I am about to do something new. See, I have already
begun! Do you not see it? I will make a pathway through
the wilderness. I will create rivers in the dry wasteland
(Isaiah 43:19).

Leadership Solutions

Six women leaders are discussing how to solve a problem. They
want to schedule a meeting with an impossible-to-reach CEO. They
all understand that the first company that connects with this person
will win a big contract. Each of the six team members has a different
leadership style. Let's listen to the conversation.

The activist leader said, "Well, someone's got to make the phone
call. I'll do that. The rest of you need to…" She was interrupted.

The strategic leader said, "Thank you. I'll take it from here.
Before you make that call, I believe that we need to make a plan."

"I agree. We need to make sure that everyone has some responsibility and works in their area of strength. Wouldn't you all agree?"
said the tactical leader.

"Excuse me, everyone. I would like to write any letters we need
written. I'll do the first draft and then we can make changes if
needed," said the creative leader.

"We just need to make sure that we use nice stationery. We have
to make a good connection. They won't open our letter if it doesn't
look nice. Maybe something with roses and ribbons," said the collaborative leader.

"Roses and ribbons are okay…if you want to go that way. But
I happen to know that the manager in that office loves chocolate
cookies. I'll bake some and send them over as a gift from us all,"
added the dramatic leader.

Each team member contributed to the process and because they
allowed each one to operate in their own, unique leadership style,
they won the contract! Each woman understood the beauty and

power of her gifts and what she brought to the table. She also understood what the others could contribute. They each brought a measure of joy to the mission they were working on together.

In order for you to have joy, you must first accept that you are a beautiful, powerful woman destined to do great things. Remember that you change the atmosphere everywhere you go. That can be a difficult task, especially since there are times when everything around you tells you just the opposite. As long as you believe that you and your leadership style are not good enough, strong enough, or stable enough to win, then the end result will be disappointment and failure. Remember, it is impossible for you to lose once you walk in the beauty and power of your leadership style!

10

Tips for Every Leader

Leadership Is Warfare!

Warfare. What images come to mind when you see the word? Does it fill you with discomfort? Does it excite you? Does it make you shout for joy? Does it make you want to run for cover?

The word *warfare* doesn't necessarily have to conjure up negative thoughts and feelings. There are times when war is necessary. There are times when the only thing you can do is fight. Great leaders understand that. They understand that there are times when the only way to gain victory is to fight a battle. Great leaders can see and smell a battle before it reaches them. They can touch victory's pulse and sense the threat of defeat if the tide of the battle changes. They understand the climate of warfare because leadership and warfare walk hand in hand.

As a woman in leadership warfare should be familiar to you. If not, let's pose a few questions. Are you in the position you've always wanted? Are you involved in strategic planning and decision-making where you work? And one of the most critical questions anyone can ask…how well do you get along with your team members and other leaders?

For many of us, this last question is the center of our leadership world. If we get along well with other leaders, then everything else in our world is easier to handle. If we have a great relationship with our supervisor and other leaders, then we can better manage any task presented because we have a built-in support network of others who understand the weight of our position. So how do we manage these challenges? How do we build bridges that can hold the weight of the leadership battleground?

You must first accept and then embrace your leadership birthright. Never let it go. Accept it. Walk in it. Embrace it. Love it. Talk about it. Dance in it. Sing in it. Lead in it. Be woman enough to acknowledge it and realize that you are already leading. You've been leading since you arrived on the planet. You've been leading since you took your first step. You are born to lead and if you choose to ignore that fact, the battle will still come to your doorstep. The battle will still come into your home, your workplace, your friendships, and your relationships. This is why you must accept the challenge and not allow the enemy to gain ground. You are born to lead, and sister…leadership is warfare!

Doing the Hip Cross

I remember my mother talking to me about being a lady. I really hated that word but it was an integral part of my mother's conversation. She had the agonizing experience of teaching me to cross my legs. My mother and her friends always crossed their legs at the hip. They looked so glamorous with those straight skirts. As I gazed on these visions of feminine perfection, I decided to master the hip cross. If this was a part of being ladylike, I would commit to learning how to sit like a pretzel and because of its beauty, I was certain I would enjoy it.

The first time I tried to do the "pretzel hip cross" I fell off the chair. I could not keep my balance long enough to stay seated. Each time I tried, I rolled over on my side with my legs, still crossed, in the air. I could not untangle my legs fast enough to keep from falling onto the floor in a tangled heap. After secretly practicing this activity with little to show for it, I decided to seek out an expert in the field, the expert leg crosser…my mother.

Hours later, after gathering my courage, I finally asked her to share her secret with me. After all, I was her daughter and if she could do it, then I could, right? After demonstrating my version of the hip cross and observing that I had not inherited her grace or her long legs, she instructed me in the art of crossing my legs at the ankle. That was fine for someone else, but it was not the counsel I expected and it did not give me the results I wanted.

When I sat down and tried it, my legs gapped open at the top. I looked like an oversized harp. I also had trouble keeping my dresses under control. Like slithering snakes, they crawled up my legs. I stood most of the time if I could get away with it just to avoid a scene. I just wanted to forget the whole thing and put on a pair of pants, but that was impossible. During this time, I couldn't wear pants to school or church so that was out of the question. Believe it or not, I did like wearing dresses, but after all the lessons, the ruffles and fluff irritated me and I still could not do the hip cross.

As I matured, I learned that crossing my legs at the hip was not the key or the secret to femininity, nor was it the key to abundant life. I am so thankful to have learned that Jesus already holds that place. My not becoming a human pretzel matters little to Him. But after many years of practice and much prayer, I have news. I can now cross my legs…at the hip!

Now, what does this have to do with leadership? It has everything to do with it. How can you lead others if you don't feel good about who you are and your abilities? I'll explain. If we take a look back at our childhoods, we will find things that make us smile, laugh, or feel sorrowful. All these things helped to make us who we are today. The challenge of learning to cross my legs readied me to climb other mountains in my life, including the challenge of leading others.

As time went on, I even grasped the true meaning of the term *ladylike*. Being a lady or a female leader in the Master's service has nothing to do with crossing my legs or keeping my hands folded in my lap. Being a feminine leader God can use has everything to do with grasping and savoring the fruit of the Spirit.

I feel joy because I am free after touching the hem of His magnificent garment. I experience peace when I give Him control of my life and my leadership abilities. Through my experiences, I learned that long-suffering is a part of life and builds character. Character helps me to see the challenges others face and to extend grace because He did the same for me.

I also learned that kindness and goodness opens the door to faithfulness if I continue to allow Him to lead me. Gentleness and self-control are integral parts of my being when I realize God is in control and He will help me when it's time for me to lead others. It is about being a vessel of honor that brings the Father glory.

My spirit, because Christ dwells in me, is strong so I cannot allow the enemy to hold me captive with a little thing like learning to cross my legs. I now know that leg crossing and other childhood challenges were for my good. I discovered that like a caterpillar, the Lord placed me in His cocoon and I emerged a godly woman leader, filled with His power. Shedding the cocoon of past experiences, I learned that I truly can do all things through Christ, who strengthens me. My legs and my leadership abilities are a witness!

> But the Holy Spirit produces this kind of fruit in our lives: love, joy, peace, patience, kindness, goodness,

faithfulness, gentleness, and self-control. There is no law against these things! (Galatians 5:22-23).

Keep the Lines of Communication Open

If you don't connect, you cannot achieve success. When your team cannot hear you, they cannot follow you. They need to see, hear, speak, touch, and experience you as a leader. Send them notes. Listen when they speak. Let them know when they have touched you. Let them see that leaders can stop and speak, listen, feel, and touch. Let them see that leaders are human too.

Let your team members know that you feel they are important.

It only takes a few minutes and a few words to inspire. What's the difference between motivation and inspiration? You can motivate someone to brush their teeth so that their teeth will not rot. But when you inspire someone, you touch something within them that continues to sing each time they think of the moment. You light an inner fire that does not go out, even after you leave their presence. How much are you willing to give up to light a fire within others?

Solicit contributions from your team.

There are few things as powerful as a leader who solicits feedback. Whenever you give your team the power to step into the arena and take ownership of the process, it changes the game. When team members believe that their opinions matter, they are more willing to assist you in doing what you need to do in order to fulfill the mission. There is nothing more powerful than ownership of the process.

Always ask questions before giving orders.

When was the last time you asked your team members' opinion about what they do? Asking questions is one the easiest ways to connect with your team. People will always surprise you if you give them the freedom to do their jobs. Ask them for ways to improve what they do and the way that they do it.

They usually know the job better because they are doing it. So go ahead and start asking questions. You will not only learn something new; you will connect with your team in a new way.

Make your team members feel important by showing your appreciation.

There are few things that touch others more powerfully than appreciation. It is one of the four most important human needs. When someone feels appreciated, they will do above and beyond what is expected without being asked.

Appreciation changes hearts, minds, and attitudes. It softens a heart hardened by past mistakes. It changes a mind once steeled by apathy. It brightens an attitude dulled by neglect. As a leader, you can overcome the past mistakes of a former leader by showing your appreciation. You soften that mind by giving that team member something to do that stimulates their intellect. You can touch that neglected attitude by giving them a task that requires tenacity. You are in charge and appreciation is one of your most powerful secret weapons.

Be enthusiastic and energized about your mission.

Enthusiasm is contagious. Even if the mission is not something that one would categorize as exciting, you can make it appear to be exciting by how you use enthusiasm. If monotony sits in the seat of leadership, then your team will become monotonous. If boredom holds you and your team captive, then discover ways to shake things up and still stay on task. If you have challenges in this area, ask your team for help. They will assist you in coming up with creative ways to complete the mission and make it more enjoyable.

If you cannot generate some enthusiasm about what you do, then it's time to do something different. The speed of the leader is the speed of the gang! Remember that you are the example so you have to lead when it comes to enthusiasm!

Watch Out

There is nothing more extraordinary than knowing how powerful you are and using the power for good and not evil. Watch who you touch. Watch what you speak. Watch what you do because there is glory in your fingertips, majesty in your words, and fire in your actions. Today, spread your mighty wings, change the world around you with your love, and watch as miracles appear.

A Focused Woman Leader

What do a focused woman leader and lightning have in common? They can both strike at any given place or at any given time without warning. That makes them both unpredictable facets of creation and they are both dangerous! Lightning lights up the sky and then hits its target with great accuracy. It leaves behind a trail of devastation in the aftermath of its deadly visit. A focused woman leader is like that lightning. She decides on a target and then strikes and takes what belongs to her. She uses her resources not to harm, but to bring joy and happiness wherever she goes. A focused woman leader understands that she must leave behind a legacy of change and success. She leaves the place where she struck richer than when she discovered it. She leaves behind the essence of her power for future generations.

The Pageant

"Everyone must eat dinner and get your baths early tonight!" While growing up, that statement signaled the beginning of what promised to be one of the most exciting events in our household. After we completed all the preparations, all female family members scrambled for a seat in front of the television.

The call went out for lights, camera, and action! Ooohs and aaahs filled each mouth. No one dared utter a word during the question-and-answer segment. No one left the room, except during the commercials. No one breathed as the announcer called the names of the finalists. Everything and everyone stood in suspended animation as stardust from TV-land clouded our eyes with tears. We made it through another magnificent moment.

This was the event that made us rush to eat our dinner, clean the kitchen, and make sure that everything in the house was in order so there would be no disturbances. This was one of those times when, even as teenagers, we avoided the telephone. This was one of life's best treasures. This was the event that we all hoped for, prayed for, and prepared for. This was...the beauty pageant.

At the end of the pageantry, we climbed into bed with our little minds saturated with the evening's splendor. How could one watch such magnificence and be expected to sleep soundly? How could any sane person not want the moments to live on forever? It was all so beautiful. Dreams of our own bathing suit parades, complete with high heels, evening gowns, long blonde hair, and blue eyes dominated our sleeping patterns. This was what life was all about, right?

During my youth, these beauty pageants were an important part of my life. I never entered or participated in these pageants. I only watched. Any pageants that came across the airwaves were high times in our house. We ate dinner early and cleared away any household chores so we could make the mad dash for the television before pageant time.

Popcorn-filled bowls and soda cans that once flew from person to person stopped in midair as they called the names of the finalists.

We became totally immersed in the sea of brilliant lights and mesmerized by the hope of dazzling beauty. We vigorously analyzed the talent competition and mercilessly examined the judges' credentials. Nothing could pollute the pleasure of our world.

Without realizing what was happening to us, society downloaded its beauty software into our spirits. Through these experiences, we learned what it meant to be beautiful in the world's eyes. We learned the accepted standards of beauty. To be considered beautiful, one must have an hourglass figure, be below average weight, and have large breasts, full hips, full calves, shoulder-length blonde hair, pearly white teeth, and flawless white skin. This was really a sad scene, especially since as African-Americans we would never reach or come close to the accepted standard of physical beauty. As a matter of fact, most of the women in America, no matter what their ethnicity, did not come close to this warped view of beauty.

Many years later, I had the opportunity to direct a beauty pageant. The original idea of this pageant was to promote the physical beauty of the participants. When the financial backers of the pageant approached me about directing this event, I pitched them the idea of hosting a different type of pageant—one for those who would most likely never enter one of the major pageants. I suggested that we host a pageant based on character and the ability to see feminine confidence on display.

The backers allowed me to redesign the format. Before the pageant started, I threw out the bathing suit competition and worked on fostering the value of sisterhood. By the time the event ended, the participants all felt like winners. They understood that this event was about more than how they looked. It was about how they felt about themselves.

What about those of us who do fit the world's mold of beauty? What about your perfect figure, your blonde, brunette, or auburn hair, and pearly white teeth? How do you manage to maintain this image of perfection? You operate under so much pressure to maintain this worldly reflection of beauty that your life seems like a pressure cooker.

This is one of the reasons women experience eating disorders and suffer under the knife of plastic surgery. It is easy to imagine that even if you do have some of the traits mentioned, you feel chained to a fate worse than death and imprisonment. This prison can keep you chained, miserable, and eventually bitter as your looks begin fading.

If your physical appearance changes, your status changes. Gain a few pounds, and you immediately start dieting. You still have to keep your hair dyed, or you lose beauty points. Everything has to be perfect. It is as if there is some huge scorecard that adds and subtracts points according to how you follow the rules. It is a never-ending cycle that eats away at your self-image.

The saddest part is that millions of women would love to be in your place. They believe that they would love to have your face, figure, skin color, and hair. They do not see or feel the pressure that holds you captive. If we are not careful to listen to the Holy Spirit, we can bow before an idol more cruel than death. An idol that demands perfection and attention. It is the idol of appearance worship.

Many of us had or still have people in our lives who seem to have something negative to say about how we look, think, or act. With our permission, they deposit bits and pieces of debris into our hearts and spirits. These deposits hurt! The debris is also difficult to clean out once deposited. The depositors may be parents, teachers, or even spouses.

The enemy does not play fairly and will use the first available vessel. He will use anyone to steal, kill, and to destroy. He especially loves using those closest to you and even those called to lead and teach you. Unfortunately, many of these people do not know that they are pawns in a horrendous game and are being used as instruments of destruction.

As humans, we are so quick to judge others. We make assumptions based on physical appearance daily. We do a quick scan and if the results of that scan please us, we accept the person. If not, we do not invite them to our tea party. What would happen if the Lord had the same standards? Most of us would be in bad shape. To put it more accurately, we would be down in a pit. Jesus Christ made the ultimate sacrifice so that we do not have to feel rejected.

Can you imagine anyone loving you so much that He would lay down His life for you? Can you imagine someone loving you so much that He would make the ultimate sacrifice so He could spend eternity with you and you with Him? Well, that is exactly what Jesus did. At first it was hard for me to accept, but as I began to spend more time with the Lord and reading His Word, my understanding of His nature grew and I gradually received it. It is just that simple. Jesus loves you so much that He died to set you free. Free from sin and death and rejection. He has placed your sin as far from you as east is from west.

Because of His sacrifice, we gained access to a royal inheritance. You are beautiful and precious to the Lord. He is a God of wonder and love. He loves us in our uniqueness. He did not make any mistakes! Sometimes we cannot see His purpose for our lives and begin to question His methods. I have found such peace in just asking Him to show me His plan for my life. Be careful if you decide to listen to His response. It may not be what you thought or wanted.

As leaders of today, we have the unique ability and opportunity to make these types of changes without excuse. We can stand and recognize the beauty of God's wonderful color, figure, personality, and femininity palettes. We can let women know that He is the Master and we are His masterpieces.

Because we are leaders, we can change the rules and level the playing field by teaching our daughters, sisters, and friends that God did not make any mistakes. He fashioned us all in the fullness of His likeness and each one of us is a daughter of the King. As leaders, we can change the rules, direct the pageants, and teach the lessons. Isn't it great being a leader the Lord can use?

So let your hair down! Freedom is here! Our Savior paid the price for us to be free, for us to embrace our beauty, for us to stand side-by-side with other women and celebrate our unique style of leadership. We are the work of the Master Potter and He did not make any mistakes...just leaders!

I Am Sienna

"You are the prettiest and smartest little thing that your Granny has ever seen," my grandmother said as she buried me in the softness of her embrace. I could feel the stiffness of the starch from her dress as it scratched my young face, but that did not matter. I was her first-born grandchild and I was in her arms. There was no other song I longed to hear and no other melody that sounded so sweet. She adored me and I adored her.

The year I turned six, my family moved from North Carolina to Okinawa, Japan, where I started the first grade. The year was 1961. Just as the Civil Rights movement was in full swing in the United States, we moved to a foreign country. Being only six, I was oblivious to all the noises of race that surrounded me. What I did not know was that ethnicity touches you wherever you go and you cannot hide who and what you are for long.

I loved the warm Okinawa sunshine and school but when I went to the second grade, things changed. Granny passed away. At first, her passing didn't seem to bother me because it had been almost two years since I had seen her. The essence of her words and the fragrance of her love still lingered and touched me in the landscape of my identity.

But something had changed. When I tried to access Granny's picture from my memory banks, the photograph was blurred. And when I looked in the mirror, I had difficulty finding that pretty, smart girl who used to stare back at me. I missed my grandmother and tried to find her each night in the folds of my pillow.

I missed Granny and did not know how to replace the comfort she gave me. So as I went to the second grade, I decided I needed something more than playing with my three younger sisters. I needed a boyfriend. I had no idea what to do with a boyfriend but it just seemed like the thing to do, especially since I had the perfect candidate.

He was beautiful. His blond hair captured each ray of light and commanded them to dance to his music. His blue eyes made you want to swim even if you had never had swimming lessons. His name was Mike and he was the most handsome boy I had ever seen. I decided that he had to be mine.

Mike sat in front of me in class. Every day he would turn around, place both arms on my desk, cradle his chin on the back of his hands, and stare into my face. The teacher had to constantly remind him to turn around because he would not do his work. He seemed to like looking at me as much as I liked looking at him.

"You are so pretty and I like you," he said. I smiled because I thought he was great too. But one day, Mike did something that would change the way I saw myself and my life forever.

"Mike, I want you to be my boyfriend," I said as I got lost in the deep blue ocean that lapped the shores of his eyes. He smiled and then shook his head, telling me his answer was no. I was startled. How could this boy—this boy who could not stop looking at me—say *no*? How could he play with my seven-year-old emotions and leave me hanging in the air of his rejection?

"Didn't you tell me that you thought I was pretty and you liked me?"

"Yes, but I can't be your boyfriend," he said without releasing me from his stare.

"But why not? Don't you like me anymore?"

"Yes, I like you but I can't be your boyfriend."

"But why not?" I pressed him for an answer and he gave it. He took his index finger and slowly rubbed the back of my hand.

I pulled my hand away and looked at it but could see nothing but the golden tone of my natural skin color. There was no dirt. I had not marked it with a pencil or crayon. It was the same hand that held my books, pencils, and crayons that I used in school. There was nothing different except for the invisible print left by his touch.

Oh, no! There must be something wrong with this boy, I thought.

"What's wrong with the back of my hand and why can't you be my boyfriend?" Ribbons of silence waved like warning flags in the airspace around my mind because of what I was about to hear.

"I can't be your boyfriend because…you are black," he said with a slight frown, withdrawing his hand

This boy is not just dumb but he's blind too! Feelings for which I had no name bubbled up into my heart and crystallized into thoughts. I had fallen in love with someone who was not only blind but also as dumb as a doorknob. I had to educate this boy.

"I am not black. I am sienna," I said in my firstborn teaching voice. I had younger sisters who had more sense than he did. And they knew their colors too. I felt certain that once he heard the truth, he would see the error of his ways, realize that he made a dumb mistake, and then become my boyfriend.

What he did not know was that when I was in the first grade, my mother promised to buy me a box of 64 crayons when I went to the second grade. When I got those crayons, the first thing I did was to find my skin color. If he was smart, he would have asked his mother to buy him a box of 64 crayons so he could have learned his colors too.

When I got my crayons, I breathed in the colors. I had to find my identity within this radiant, vibrant palette. I had to find my skin color. There it was. It was beautiful, rich, creamy sienna. It was a far cry from the black crayon this silly boy was talking about.

"No, you are black," he said with some irritation in his voice. Well, I had already found his color, so I was ready for him.

"So, what color are you if you think I am black?"

"I am white!" he said with a harshness I had never heard in his voice before.

Okay, so this boy really is blind and dumb too. I am so glad that he did not want to be my boyfriend. He doesn't even know his colors! my mind screamed with seven-year-old rage. How did he get to second grade without knowing his colors? I was more than prepared to give him a lesson in color education that day.

As I reached into my 64 colors, I knew that I had the crayon for him and it was far from white.

"You are not white! You are salmon pink! See, here it is," I said as I placed the crayon next to back of his hand so he could see the perfect match.

"I am not pink but you are black!" he said with teary eyes. As he turned around, I caught sight of his face as it turned red with anger.

The back of his head was foreign to me. For the first time, I could see the thick, greasiness of his hair. For the first time, I could see the largeness of his ears. He was not so handsome anymore. He was dumb and I wanted nothing else to do with him. That afternoon, I decided that I needed to have a talk with my mother regarding this pink boy.

I usually enjoyed my ride home on the bus but that day, the thoughts of my conversation with Mike kept me from seeing the beauty of the shining China Sea and the luscious, green leaves of banana tress that dotted the wondrous landscape of the island. I was focused on talking to my mother, the only person I believed would have the answers I needed.

The familiar sound of fans humming greeted me as I came in the front door. The smell of dinner cooking in the kitchen embraced me and the safety of my bedroom called to me as I ran down the hallway. I threw my book bag on the bed and kicked off my shoes. I wanted to throw them against the wall and scream because I did not understand the feelings that burned inside me.

"Hi, baby. How was school today?" My mother's voice cut through my focus as I ran to her and hugged her.

"Mama, a boy in my class called me a name today. He told me that I was black. Look at me, Mama. What color do you see? Can't you tell that I am not black? I am sienna," I said as I pulled away so that she could get a good look at me. I saw the sides of her mouth trying to form a smile although she tried to hide it.

"Baby, they call us *black* and *colored*," she replied, not looking up as she pulled a sky blue towel from the pile of clothes on the bed.

"Well, Mama, who is *they*?" I wanted to find these people and have a talk with them. The first thing I wanted to do was to buy them a box of 64 crayons because "they" obviously needed help with their colors too.

"Baby, there are many things you do not understand yet," Mama said. "They call us many things, including the name *Negro*. There are also a few other names they call us that I won't mention." As she stared out the window I saw an expression take over her face that I had never seen before.

"Negro? Mama, I don't like the sound of that word," I shrugged my defiant shoulders and sat on the edge of the bed.

"Well, baby, there will be a lot of things in this life that you will not like. This is just one of them."

I walked away before she could say more. A strange lump was forming in my throat. I had heard enough on this subject for the day.

Mama had never taught me about differences. For the first time, I realized that I was the only black girl in my class. For the first time, I realized that although I was smart, the other children in my class, including Mike, had always known something about me that I had just discovered. Maybe I wasn't so smart after all. One finger had opened up a whole new way of looking at the world…and the world looking back at me.

> What lies behind us and what lies ahead of us are tiny matters compared to what lives within us.
>
> —Oliver Wendell Holmes

This story of identity had a great impact on my personal journey to destiny. Over the years, I've discovered that identity has everything to do with destiny. There have been times when not understanding destiny robbed me of much. There have been missed opportunities because I did not see myself as worthy or good enough or smart enough or anything else enough. Many of those feelings of inadequacy stemmed from other events like the one with Mike.

But the one finger incident did not have its full intended impact on my life. Instead of sitting down and accepting defeat, I became defiant whenever someone tried to tell me or make me feel that I was anything less than beautiful and smart. I had to fight this battle not only with others but also within myself. Even though I was young when this happened, I began to understand the pain of being rejected because of *what* I was instead of *who* I was. I became aware of how others treated me because of my skin color and personality. I watched and waited to be rejected and blamed many of my life's failures on the behavior of others. For many years, I allowed this incident to color my world with a murky darkness that shaped my behavior.

I made many mistakes along the way, but then something wonderful happened. I had a Road to Damascus experience in which God's light illuminated the darkness that tried to overtake me. I met the One who created me and my sienna.

He let me know that He had plans to give me a future and hope. He let me know that I was a royal daughter all glorious. He let me know that His intent was for me to discover my identity, grasp my purpose, and step into my destiny. Nothing could change that. And to think that it all began with that finger, laced with the toxicity of racism, that pointed me to destiny.

I learned that even something negative can catapult you to a place of personal power. I've learned that our identity or how we see ourselves has a great impact on how we make decisions, how we interact with others, and how we view the world. I've heard people say that if you place too much focus on identity then you are selfish and self-centered. I've heard some of the same people say that if you hold onto hurt feelings then you are prideful and just want attention.

I say that it's easy to say those things once you have found your true identity and are walking in a place of confidence. It's easy to talk about how we should be or act once we've discovered how we should be or act. But if you are still in the place where your identity is not clear, you may feel like you're caught in a time warp and still need help crossing over into the land of freedom. There are times when you just need a little help to help you get over.

Now that I've crossed over and understand the beauty and power of how God created me, I can see that those crayons helped me to solve a riddle that has plagued mankind for centuries. I can see that I have a godly obligation to help others who may be trapped on the other side of identity. I have to let them know that if I made it, they can too.

Through the innocence of youth, I also discovered the splendor of God's color palette and loved it from the moment I saw it. I am a sienna daughter of the King, a woman of African descent, living in a place that may not appreciate my skin tone, personality, or gifts. But that doesn't change the fact that God created me in His image. Nothing could change my experience with my crayon box. Not even Mike.

Step

Step into a new season. Step into the light and see shadows disappear. When you step, it changes your vision. Transition is always challenging, even when it's necessary for our personal and professional growth. Step into the arena without excuse and know that whatever challenges you face, you will be victorious. Had you not taken that step, you would remain unchanged, unempowered, and unsuccessful in your quest for change. When you stop looking at what you fear and realize that it should fear you, you become unstoppable!

Fly

Have you ever had something good happen to you and then someone tells you that it really isn't a big deal? They clip your wings and tell you to stay grounded, to be realistic, to sit in the shadow of doubt and be grateful that darkness wants your company. They mean you no good because they are stuck in yesterday's rain. They have forgotten what it feels like to fly, to live in the light and play in the sunshine. They have forgotten that they once had wings. So remember that you still have the ability to fly. Just stay away from wing clippers. They don't understand the power of the wind!

11

There Is Greatness in You

Isn't it exciting to know that God has not forgotten about us? He knows everything about us because He created us. He placed greatness inside you and He wants you to use it. He wants you to spread your wings and fly.

The challenge with greatness is that it usually stays inside of a person and will not reveal itself until it is needed. It reminds me of war. Soldiers prepare before they go to war. Their minds must be sharp so that they will follow orders without question. Their lives and the lives of their fellow soldiers depend on that. Their bodies must be fit. They physically train until their bodies respond without hesitation. Their bodies must be fit for battle. They train with their weapons until they are familiar with every rivet. They train and practice until every facet of warfare becomes second nature to them.

Once they arrive on the battlefield, their training automatically activates and they fight. Each warrior knows one thing: They will never know how powerful they are until they get into a good fight. It's the same with you. You will never know the power of your leadership style until you embrace it and walk in it. The Proverbs 31 Woman can help us all do that. She is the example of feminine leadership and when we read about her, we read about ourselves. We discover the power of the feminine facet of the Body of Christ.

Here is an overview of each leadership style and how that style flows with the others to paint a picture our Father loves.

The Activist Leader: The Hands of the Body

Have you noticed that whenever there is a project that you jump in and start before others have time to think? You are the first one to roll up your sleeves and get the party started. One of your pet peeves is hearing complaints. Complaining drains the atmosphere. Some of your sisters like to stand around and talk or complain about what is to be done, but not you. Your activist leadership spirit can barely stand complaints. "Just get the work done, and we can all go home," is your working theme. Complaining, gossiping, and any other negative conversation is not a part of who you are and what you do.

> She extends a helping hand to the poor and opens her arms to the needy (Proverbs 31:20).

You have a special place in your heart for the needy. You are drawn to the suffering. Organizing projects that benefit that group are your specialty. For you, giving of your time, energy, and possessions is like breathing. You are the one who will start a clothing drive, feed the hungry, or coordinate a fundraiser for a women's shelter.

If there is no shelter, you make it your business to develop the project. You approach business leaders and ensure that they give to your cause. You are so gifted that you may have several options and buildings to choose from once you start your campaign.

Your fire for those less fortunate than yourself shines through in all you do. In activist leadership style, you get the job done and will not rest until the shelter is furnished and women and their children have a place to live in peace and safety.

> She carefully watches everything in her household and suffers nothing from laziness (Proverbs 31:27).

There is never any dispute that you are a burst of energy. You work from sunup to sundown, many times without taking a break. While completing a project is important, it is also important to take care of yourself so you can continue doing the work of the Lord. Stop, take a deep breath, and smell the roses once in a while.

> Reward her for all she has done. Let her deeds publicly declare her praise (Proverbs 31:31).

You are most pleased with completed projects. Loose ends do not agree with your leadership style and you wish others could see and feel the joy of a task completed. Functioning as the hands, you soar to excellence by staying connected with your sisters in the feminine facet.

The Strategic Leader: The Head of the Body

You are gifted at administration and planning. You are the head and the eyes of the feminine facet, but not the brain. God supplies the brainpower, helps you to develop strategies for your life, and instructs you in the administration of those strategies.

You are also gifted at helping others develop strategies for success. You understand the power of writing things down and then watching as writing charges the atmosphere with purpose. Your heart yearns for others to experience this power so that it becomes a part of their lifestyle. Once it becomes a part of their life, it will change everything around them for good.

One of your challenges is relying on the strength of your abilities. When you rely on your own abilities and choose not to have a balanced prayer life, you can appear to be bossy and overbearing. Don't forget to include the Father in all your decisions and processes.

He is the ultimate planner and understands who you are and how you operate. He knows that you want everyone to plan their work and work their plan. If this doesn't happen, then the end result is unnecessary irritation. Give your irritation and need for control to Him. He's got your back and wants you to walk in your leadership style with ease.

> She makes sure her dealings are profitable; her lamp burns late into the night (Proverbs 31:18).

When there is work to be done, you are the ultimate organizer. Women with your leadership style usually possess the gift of financial management. Even if this is not one of your strengths, you still have an astute business mind and can see how projects should flow. You have the gift of seeing how a business should operate and can see where and how to use its resources wisely.

If you encounter challenges, you are the first to look for experts to assist you. You don't mind asking for help because for you, it is critical that all details be managed.

There are times when exhaustion pulls you into his arms and you continue working. Stop and rest. You are good but not good enough to work while exhausted. It dulls your gifts and hinders your ability to make good decisions. It also causes you to miss details. So take care of your physical self too. It will help to keep you and your gifts sharp.

> She goes to inspect a field and buys it; with her earnings she plants a vineyard (Proverbs 31:16).

Your function in the body is order and structure. When the need for a project arises, you are the consummate organizer. One might hear you say, "Let's see, Brenda, we need you to do this…and Susan, we need you to do that." It sometimes appears that you are bossy. Try and remember that everyone has a purpose, and their purpose may not be the same as yours. But also remember that we are all here to lift up the name of Jesus and to glorify God. Remember to exercise wisdom balanced with kindness.

> When she speaks, her words are wise, and she gives instructions with kindness (Proverbs 31:26).

Your heart's desire is to see that all things are done decently and in order. One thing you must always remember is that you function as the head, not the brain. The Holy Spirit already has that position covered. When addressing your order issues, remember that your sisters' priorities and marching orders are usually different. Sometimes you may have to relax your strategic priorities so things can be accomplished and others will willingly work with you to complete the mission. You need the help of your sisters to get things done. Remember, you cannot fulfill your destiny alone.

Functioning as the head and the eyes of the feminine facet, you soar to strategic leadership heights.

The Tactical Leader: The Neck and Shoulders of the Body

When there is a work to be done, you always find the power source. You are the perfect operations manager because you understand execution of a vision.

Your first questions are always, "Who is in charge? How does the system work? Who decided that things would be done this way?" Finding the source for resources and decision-making is your strength, but it can also become your area of challenge.

This trait acts as your strength when you keep in mind that your Father is really the One in charge. He opens doors no man can close and closes doors no man or woman can open. You can walk into a situation that appears to be totally chaotic and God will send His wind and destroy all the debris before you even get there.

Likewise, if you rely on your strengths and your own power, He can allow you to be in that same situation and you will have to do all the cleanup on your own. You will spend unnecessary time and energy doing something that He didn't have in mind for you to do simply because you proceeded without Him.

Remember that your presence and presentation can be over-whelming, so watch how you present yourself to others. You mean well but others may not always be able to see that once you come into their atmosphere asking direct questions.

One weakness you may experience is that you seek out the favor of influential people and begin to respect people only for what they can give or bring to the table. In other words, you look for influen-tial people so you can connect with them. It may cause you to look down on others who may not have access to similar resources.

Remember that God wants you to have favor. He just wants you to remember that all favor, even favor with men and women, comes through Him. And He has a purpose and a plan once you gain that favor. It is not so others can be exalted to a place of degrading oth-ers or making others feel badly about themselves.

She is energetic and strong, a hard worker (Proverbs 31:17).

You are strong in presence and in spirit. There are times when others misunderstand and misinterpret your actions and motives. They do not know that your real heart's desire is to please the Father and them too, if you can. You also want to have strong connections with your sisters. Isolation is not your friend, although you spend time alone because of being misunderstood. This is not God's plan for you. He knows that you need others surrounding you. Just stop, look and listen...to God.

God is faithful to send other women who need you and your gifts and they will not be threatened by your presence and presentation.

Ask the Father for wisdom. God will use your strengths and will bless you to have women around you who love you and who will understand the call on your life.

He stands ready to bless you for this task and for the battle. Just remember that you are His tactical warrior-leader, and there is nothing that can change that.

> Her husband is well known at the city gates, where he sits with the other civic leaders (Proverbs 31:23).

If you are married, you do all within your power to support and encourage your husband while still remaining true to who you are. Exhortation and encouragement reign in your marriage. You flow like no other leader in this area. Remember that while it is great to flow in these areas, ask the Holy Spirit for guidance in regulating the flow. It can be overwhelming to a more reserved mate.

> She is clothed with strength and dignity, and she laughs without fear of the future (Proverbs 31:25).

As a tactical leader, you have a strong sense of justice. You sacrifice everything for justice. You go out of your way to ensure that everyone is treated fairly. It is not unusual for you to lead and encourage groups to change a law or regulation. If there is a policy at work that you don't like, you won't stop until you see it fixed.

Remember to do your research before becoming engulfed in one of your crusades. Your husband and family will thank you for it.

Walking fully in your function as the neck and shoulders of the feminine facet, you soar to tactical leadership heights.

The Creative Leader: The Arms and Back of the Body

Your work-theme questions are, "How does this affect the people? How is the group affected? Why don't we try something different this year?" You love the thrill of helping God's people thrive.

You can see conflict before it arrives and you can feel the flow of tension before it has the chance to settle into the workings of a group.

Your challenge is helping others to see it. Oftentimes others do not want to listen and would rather stay locked in battle. You have little patience for this attitude. You would rather just leave and go on to the next adventure with another group. This is something you cannot do.

God will give you the same script with the next group so that you will learn the lesson He wants to teach you. Stand firm. Do not leave. God needs for you to stay and contribute even if they appear not to listen. Before things are finished, they will be seeking out your assistance if you stand still. Just be ready and hang your "I told you so" coat in the closet.

> Her hands are busy spinning thread, her fingers twisting
> fiber (Proverbs 31:19).

You are gifted at creating new ways to do old things. Recycling is nothing new to you. You are the woman who understands the power of the rejected. In other words, you can take someone who others felt had no value and help them to see their worth. You allow them to work with you until they get on their feet and then you send them off into a world made new.

You supply them with the necessary resources to be successful. Whatever you have is theirs. Whatever you do, you share the experience. You teach them the importance of valuing others in intangible and tangible ways so that they can pass it on to others. You live with the "pay it forward" mentality because it's just what you do.

> She finds wool and flax and busily spins it (Proverbs
> 31:13).

You have a knack for taking nothing and making something out of it. Old drapes become new tablecloths. Old silverware becomes jewelry. You take things others discard and turn them into income, generating projects from which all can benefit.

> She makes belted linen garments and sashes to sell to the merchants (Proverbs 31:24).

You are the leader who discovers new talent. You are able to see into the heart of a person and observe their hidden gifts. You understand that creative gifts are sometimes abandoned or mislabeled and discarded. But you can see and then you act. Working with the activist leader, you help to start a shelter. You mend and create clothing. You pass on your creativity and show women how to stretch their wardrobes and resources. You do whatever is necessary to mend the brokenhearted and set the captives free.

Staying in your position as the arms and back of the feminine facet, you show the world your creative leadership beauty.

The Collaborative Leader: The Heart and Torso of the Body

Your work-theme questions are: "How can we collaborate on this? Who has the talent to do this portion of the project? Where can we find the means or the person to do this? Do you know anyone who can help with this?"

You are concerned about making and keeping strong connections. Harmony is your usual theme. You are the one who never forgets birthday, anniversaries, or the personal successes of others. You are also a gifted social chairperson.

> She is like a merchant's ship, bringing her food from afar. She gets up before dawn to prepare breakfast for her household and plan the day's work for her servant girls (Proverbs 31:14-15).

You understand the need for others to fit in and are willing to work tirelessly to ensure that everyone feels comfortable in their space. Although you understand that you cannot please and care for everyone, you are willing to do what is necessary to do something rather than nothing. As hard as you try, you just cannot ignore the needs of others.

You are the ultimate diplomat. Even when you reach the executive ranks in your leadership position, you still have a heart for those serving the organization in a different level and function. You form committees to give them a voice. You review the promotion and recognition system to ensure that is fairly executed. You do all that is within the scope of your collaborative power to ensure that everyone is served fairly and justly.

You are a gift to the body and flow. Your collaborative spirit helps others to soar to new heights with the Father.

The Dramatic Leader: The Hips and Legs of the Body

You are the one who always knows what is going on within the organization, but may not say anything. Your leadership-theme questions are, "What's our next mission? What does success look like, and who is going to hold our banner?" You believe in doing things in a big way. Projects are all or nothing for you. You love being able to access resources and you don't mind sharing them with others.

You are a busy leader, but you have the ability to care for your family and friends in unique ways. You study them and ensure they have what they need.

She has no fear of winter for her household, for everyone has warm clothes (Proverbs 31:21).

Your first priority is comfort. If you cannot find what you like, you will make it or find someone who can make what you like. Fine linens, beautiful clothing, and lavish jewelry are your trademarks. Although you like these things, you will just as easily give them away to others. People are more important to you than things.

> She makes her own bedspreads. She dresses in fine linen
> and purple gowns (Proverbs 31:22).

You carry the body where it needs to go. Where the hips and legs go, the body follows. You are the facet of the body that is always in front to open doors.

You have no problem helping others become successful. You just don't want them trying to stop you. You stand out and God uses your dramatic presence to open doors for others. You don't mind this as long as they don't try and close the door in your face once they get in. All you ask is that they remember you and be considerate. You deserve consideration and when they bless you, the blessings flow back into their lives like a river!

> Reward her for all she has done. Let her deeds publicly
> declare her praise (Proverbs 31:30).

Your very presence may bring out envy in other women because you are very comfortable with your femininity. You have no problem using it to get in doors or to obtain resources you need for your mission. Don't give this much thought because one way or another, your sisters will need you. They will need you to help them gain access to places, people, and things. So relax and walk in the beauty of your leadership style.

Just stay in step with the Father as the hips and legs of the feminine facet and you will guide the body to new heights.

> Who can find a virtuous and capable wife? She is more
> precious than rubies (Proverbs 31:10).

Virtue is strength, force, an army, wealth, goods, might, power, and ready for war. Whew! I wonder how any one of us could stand alone and call ourselves virtuous.

Our real power or strength comes when we work together as the feminine facet. The end result of that coming together or that agreement is virtue, the likes of which the enemy cannot penetrate. This is the real power of a feminine leader.

> Her husband can trust her, and she will greatly enrich his life. She brings him well/not harm, all the days of her life (Proverbs 31:11-12).

We all play a part in helping each other have successful marriages. Even if we are single, we can still pray for married women. Too many of our sisters suffer in silence. They believe that if they are in pain, then it must be something they've done to bring that pain into their lives. They believe that God would not allow them to suffer if they are following His word and obeying His command.

This is so far from the truth. God knows that we all suffer at one time or another in our lives. The Bible tells us that suffering is a part of this life. But to be in obvious, self-inflicted pain or an abusive situation is far from God's truth.

As women leaders, we can exhort and encourage one another. We can pray for one another like never before. We can stand and intercede for those of us who are married. Stand and intercede for single women so they can withstand the challenges they face. Stand together so that we can serve as sisters, mothers, and friends to one another.

We can pray that women will impact their children in such a positive way that the children will rise up and love and bless them, that their husbands will appreciate them and let them know that they appreciate them and accept them as gifts to the family.

> Her children stand and bless her. Her husband praises her (Proverbs 31:28).

It sounds easy but we all know it's challenging. But once we understand who we are and how we operate, we can better appreciate our position and the position of other women. Once we understand our feminine power, we will stand, pray, walk, and move differently. We will understand that our enemy does not want us to hear the thunder of our footsteps as we move together in unity as the Virtuous Woman.

Fine-Tuned

> There are many virtuous and capable women in the world, but you surpass them all! (Proverbs 31:29).

Here is the part of this revelation that blessed me the most. It comes in verse 29. When Scripture says, "There are many virtuous and capable women in the world…" it is speaking individually to each woman. God has done many works and He is pleased with your individual deeds. In your individual works or life, you have proven yourself to be capable and strong. In other words, Linda, you have done well. Cheryl, you have done well. Gail, you have done well. Kathleen, you have done well. Every woman has gone as far as she can go on her own.

The next portion of the verse that says, "but you surpass them all!" speaks to the body collectively. Corporately, the works we (the feminine facet of the body) perform excel any individual work and bring Him the most glory. You give Him glory when you are obedient and do what He tells you to do. His desire is for us to strive for individual excellence as individual women, but we can only attain the excellence portrayed by the Proverbs 31 Woman when working in harmony and walking and moving in unity with our sisters. This, I believe, is His wonderful plan.

A body is only as good as its members. As He is fine-tuning you as an individual woman, He is also fine-tuning the feminine facet of the body of Christ. If He fine-tunes and polishes you for His work, then you also bring that polish and fine-tuning to the feminine facet of His gorgeous, lovely diamond. Isn't that good news! Don't you just love the freedom this revelation brings?

When we walk in the beauty and power of our leadership styles and then work collectively with other women, together we form the feminine facet of His body and He sees the Virtuous Woman!

Taking the Mountain

Just as there is a feminine facet of the body of Christ, there is also a male facet. Men have a similar mission. As we already know, society views and treats men differently from women. They grow up learning to depend on one another. When they are very young, we place them in team sports, where they learn the team concept.

As young girls we attend dance classes and piano lessons, where the prettiest and most talented become the lead dancers and the best students receive the most praise at recitals. This is changing but we still have challenges in this area.

From the very beginning, society feeds us heaping piles of unhealthy competition. Society teaches male children that when they win, it is as part of a team. They love and embrace competition in a different format. Men are encouraged to give their best effort to help the team win. From this mix of masculinity, the best and brightest emerge. Others pay homage to and cheer for these bright stars, for the most part without life-destroying envy.

Here is a little story that illustrates this point. There is a wealthy man who has grown old and tired. His only joy is sitting on his deck and looking at the beautiful view of the mountains and trees that surround his mansion. There is an extremely high mountain that he mentally climbs every day. He decides that he wants someone to climb this mountain and he will pay to see it done. He approaches a man by the name of Robert. He offers Robert $250,000 to climb the mountain. He makes the same offer to Jennifer. Neither Robert nor Jennifer knows the first thing about mountain climbing.

Robert knows a man named Lewis. Lewis and Robert do not get along. As a matter of fact, they avoid each other and have very little in common. Robert knows that Lewis is an expert mountain climber and loves a challenge. Robert does not hesitate to ask Lewis for assistance. He offers him $25,000 plus expenses for his trouble and Lewis agrees to what he sees as lucrative terms. The men begin to plan their adventure.

Jennifer knows a woman named Kathy. Jennifer and Kathy are not on speaking terms. They stopped speaking for some reason that has been long forgotten by both of them, yet they continue in darkness. Kathy is an expert mountain climber, yet Jennifer refuses to ask Kathy for assistance. Jennifer scours the countryside looking for someone to help her with this challenge. She exhausts her energies and wastes valuable time looking for a resource that she already has. By the time she finally decides to ask Kathy, the men have already started the climb. When she and Kathy finally come to terms and start the planning, the men have already taken the mountain!

This story is the perfect illustration of how we, as women, can be our own worst enemies. We need to learn how to get out of our flesh and walk in and with the Holy Spirit. Just because we do not like someone does not mean that we should avoid them or not give them an opportunity to be blessed. Our Lord faced and dealt with people who hated Him on a daily basis. What did He do? He endured and blessed. The true test of your character is not how you treat someone you like, but rather how you treat someone you dislike! It is easy to show kindness to someone who is kind to you.

Let's take another look at this Proverbs 31 Woman. Here is a verse I found to be quite interesting:

> She is like a merchant's ship, bringing her food from afar. She gets up before dawn to prepare breakfast for her household and plan the day's work for her servant girls (Proverbs 31:14-15).

This woman gets up while it is still dark and begins her daily routine. But wait, am I reading these verses correctly? This woman had servant girls! That means that she did not do everything alone. I truly believe this is a wonderful revelation for most of us. She and her team did everything together. She did not even get up at night alone. I love it! She had help from other women!

Unity is the glue that holds things together. We can imagine that, just like in the households of today, there was cooking, cleaning and other household duties. Isn't it nice when someone offers to help with the household chores? What this verse is clearly saying is that when we women all work together, we are pleasing to our Father and accomplish much for the Kingdom of God.

The Lord is coming back for a bride composed of individuals who have been woven together into one body, working together as one. If you pull one thread, the entire garment unravels. The Body of Christ is like that fabric. Every individual must possess the spirit of a bride individually, and then be woven into the body collectively. We are woven into the body by one common thread more precious than gold. This thread is the blood of Jesus, the most powerful substance in the universe. If one removes or pulls that thread, the entire piece of fabric falls apart.

This is the purpose of the Proverbs 31 Woman. She shows us that with the help of our sisters, we can do what seems impossible. We cannot do it alone. Even Jesus proved that by His example. He chose twelve men to work with Him. Although He knew that they were all less than perfect, He chose them. Although He knew that they were less than loyal, He worked with them. Although He knew that they were less then valiant, He died for them.

We must follow His example if we are His bride. Only then can we come together and do what He has called us to do. Only then can we truly don our royal robes and serve Him and our sisters as leaders.

Have you have read this book and realized that you need a change in your life? Do you want to know that you will spend eternity in heaven with the Lord? If you answered yes, the following prayer and verses of Scripture hold the key to your eternal future and will help you start your journey.

All persons who live now, all those who lived in the past, and all who will live in the future need a Savior. Jesus came to earth so that we could have life and have that life more abundantly. Pray this prayer and you have His promise that He will become Lord of your life and give you the gift of eternal life.

Lord, I confess that I am a sinner and I need a Savior. Father, please forgive me for my sins. I believe that You sent Your Son Jesus to die on the cross at Calvary, where He shed His precious blood. I believe that on the third day, He rose from the dead and He is now seated at Your right hand, making intercession for me. I ask You now, Lord Jesus, to take control and become Lord of my life so that I can live with You for all eternity. I thank You for the precious gift of salvation.

If you confess with your mouth that Jesus is Lord and believe in your heart that God raised him from the dead, you will be saved (Romans 10:9).

If you prayed that prayer, the angels in heaven are throwing a heavenly party. Jesus said, "There is joy in the presence of God's angels when even one sinner repents" (Luke 15:10). Please write and let us share in your joy of this newfound life in Christ Jesus.

Dr. Gail Hayes
PO Box 71312
Durham, NC 27722
www.handleyourbusinessgirl.com

Gail M. Hayes has served as a consultant to women in the workplace by helping them to improve their relationships and become agents of change. Because of her passion for helping working women (whether they are working on an assembly line, making power decisions from the board room, or standing at a diaper-changing table), she developed the Handle Your Business Girl Empowerment Network, empowering women who want to make connections with other women.

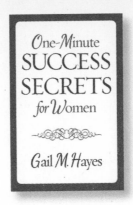

One-Minute Success Secrets for Women
By Gail M. Hayes

Women who want to find success and live with purpose will find the help they need in *One-Minute Success Secrets for Women*. Popular speaker and author Gail M. Hayes is dedicated to empowering women to pursue success in their work, relationships, and spiritual lives. In her new book she offers spiritually grounded wisdom and inspiration that makes it possible for women to...

- leave behind bitterness and strife
- face their fears of vulnerability
- find purpose in community
- embrace their God-given dreams
- take risks and silence doubts

Each nugget of wisdom can be digested in just a minute, making this the perfect book for the busy professionals, wives, and moms who have to make the most of every minute they can!

To learn more about Harvest House books and
to read sample chapters, log on to our website:

www.harvesthousepublishers.com

HARVEST HOUSE PUBLISHERS
EUGENE, OREGON